What Happened

from the

Cross to the Throne

T0204382

Should have been written 400 years ago.

By

E.W. KENYON

E.W. KENYON
Author

Eighteenth Printing

Printed in U.S.A.

Copyright 1998

by

KENYON'S GOSPEL PUBLISHING SOCIETY

ISBN 1-57770-001-5

FIRST WORDS

HIS book will blaze a new path in constructive interpretation of the Pauline revelation.

It uncovers many new veins of primary truths long covered by sense knowledge interpretation of the Word.

The first ten or twelve chapters deal with the legal side of the plan of redemption.

It shows what God did in Christ from the incarnation until He sat down at the right hand of the Majesty on High.

It gives a brief summary of what the incarnation had within it.

The earth walk of the man reveals the fact that Israel had Jehovah on their hands.

The Author of the covenant, the law, the sacrifices, the One who had appointed the priesthood and the great day of atonement, was in their midst and they did not recognize Him.

The tragedy of the garden scene, where angels strengthened and comforted the rejected Jehovah, the incarnate Son of God.

The trial with its bitter jealousy, its deception and dishonesty, where the God of the Old Covenant was spit upon, reviled and cast out by the very people He had brought into being.

The cross with its agonies, where the hero God man became sin.

Perhaps the strangest feature of it all, was that not one person knew that He was dying for their sins, that He was bearing the penalty of their transgressions.

Three days of gloom and darkness settled over the hearts of the disciples, the kingdom dreams were ended. They did not understand where the Master had gone or what He was suffering.

They were staggered by His resurrection. They were mystified by the forty days before His ascension.

They did not know He had carried His blood into the heavenly Holy of Holies.

Neither was it known that He had delivered the Old Testament Saints from Paradise when He ascended from Mount Olivet.

They little appreciated the fact that the cloud that received Him out of their sight was the Old Testament Saints being taken to the Father's house.

They did not know He was to sit down at the right hand of the Majesty on High.

The legal part of the work of redemption had been completed and now the vital could begin in the upper room.

Much of this will be new to you, but I want you to read it with an open mind.

It has transforming power enwrapped within it.

Many believe that this message is a forerunner of a great outpouring of the Holy Spirit with a revival such as the nation has never known.

It would be beautiful if it were the ushering in of the last days.

If you have not read any of my other books, and your heart is hungering for a clearer knowledge of your rights and privileges in Christ, we urge you to feast upon them.

This book contains many repetitions; however, it is unavoidable, as the subjects would be incomplete without them.

Chapter I

STRUGGLE FOR FAITH

HE faith problem is becoming very acute.

Waves of unbelief are sweeping over the church.

Many of our leaders have been swept into the whirlpool of modernism.

Earnest thinkers are seeking for a solution.

The greater percentage of the devotional writings of the past century are from the pens of the mystics.

Today there is a demand for a definite, well defined path that the bewildered minds of this troubled age may find their way into the realm of faith.

A new investigation of the Pauline Revelation is demanded.

The question is being asked by many, "Have we had the whole truth?"

Did the pioneers like Luther, Calvin, Arminius and the Wesleys have the whole truth?

We reverence these men for what they have given us.

There has been far too little growth in the knowledge of the Pauline Revelation since their day.

Here is a new approach to the heart of Redemption.

It is an answer to the question, "What happened from the cross to the seating of the Master on the right hand of the Majesty on High?"

We believe that the age of sense knowledge doctrines is past.

Christianity is not in its dotage, it is more virile than any of the thinkers have recognized.

It has within it the solution for the human problem.

Christianity has the vitality and ability of God.

The Pauline Revelation has the solution for the faith problem.

When I discovered that the apostles who were in close companionship with the Master knew nothing of the real mission of the man, I was staggered.

They did not know what happened at the Incarnation, the fact is they did not know that it was an Incarnation.

If Mary did tell them what had taken place, they received it as an idle tale of a fond mother.

When they stood about the cross and watched the death throes of the Man who was hanging there, they did not know that He was Jehovah, the God of Abraham, Isaac and Jacob.

Israel was crucifying the blood covenant Partner of Abraham and they were ignorant of it.

When Jesus commanded them to tarry until the spirit came, they did not understand what was going to happen.

They had followed the wonder Man; yet who He was, why He

11

came, what He was to suffer, and what they were to gain by His suffering, was all unknown to them.

They did not know what happened on the cross, or during the three days and nights before His resurrection, but we must know of these three days, for this is the thing that will build faith in us. The mystery is hidden in these three days.

I wonder if we dare face the facts as they actually are.

If you could eliminate all you know about Jesus from the Pauline epistles and go back with me now and stand before the cross with John, Peter, Mary and the others; if we could be as ignorant of who He was, and the reason for His death on the cross as they were, I think we might appreciate the unveiling that the Father gave to Paul.

The disciples did not know the Man as a Substitute.

They could not comprehend what was going to take place in the upper room.

Chapter II

ESTABLISHED IN RIGHTEOUSNESS

IGHTEOUSNESS is the key word in Paul's epistles. It means the ability to stand in the Father's presence without the sense of fear, condemnation, or inferiority. Here is a promise of it.

Isaiah 54:13-14. "And all thy children shall be taught of Jehovah; and great shall be the peace of thy children. In righteousness shall they be established: thou shalt be far from oppression, for thou shalt not fear; and from terror, for it shall not come near thee."

The greatest blessing of the New Creation is to be established in righteousness, to acquire a righteousness consciousness.

We have a sin consciousness.

We have had a weakness consciousness that has kept us slaves of fear.

As a nation, we have tax consciousness and will have it for generations to come.

But what a sense of victory, of freedom would be ours if we knew that we were the righteousness of God and were established in that fact.

Sin consciousness has made slaves of the human race.

It has destroyed the initiative in multitudes.

It has been the oldest and most persistent enemy of faith.

You cannot have faith in the Word when you are under condemnation.

You see righteousness means the ability to stand in the presence of God.

What would sonship be worth if we did not have righteousness?

The Father would have no pleasure in His children because they would be shrinking, cowardly, fearful beings.

The children would never enjoy the Father's presence.

No redemption would be worth the name that did not include righteousness.

No New Creation and sonship would be worth the title, if righteousness did not become a part of it.

So the object of the redemption that God wrought in His Son was to make man righteous.

That was the ultimate objective of the Father.

He dared to make His Son a Substitute for the human race.

We were bankrupt, sold out to the adversary, hopeless.

Ephesians 2:12 describes it, "That ye were at that time separate from Christ, alienated from the commonwealth of Israel, and strangers from the covenants of the promise, having no hope, and without

God in the world."

Hopeless, Godless, but here.

God now lays upon His precious Son the iniquities of us all.

He not only pays the penalty of our transgression, but He conquers our enemy and master, Satan, and strips him of his authority; then makes re-creation a possibility on legal grounds.

Now God can give to man eternal life, His own nature.

He drives out of man the old nature, the old self; and He gives him a new self, a new nature.

Man becomes a new species as one translates II Cor. 5:17.

The old man that is recreated is the human spirit.

Then God renews his mind, bringing it into subjection to this recreated spirit.

The new man gains the ascendancy over the senses, or the physical body, and becomes a master of himself in Christ.

This new man now has become the righteousness of God in Christ.

II Cor. 5:21. "Him who knew no sin he made to be sin on our behalf; that we might become the righteousness of God in him."

You see, we become righteous by receiving a new nature.

Israel had righteousness reckoned to them, set to their account, but the new creation has God Himself as their righteousness

Romans 3:26. "That he himself might be righteous and the righteousness of him who has faith in Jesus." (Mar.)

Not only does the Father Himself become our sponsor and our righteousness, but in I Cor. 1:30 we read, "But of him are ye in Christ Jesus, who was made unto us wisdom from God, and righteousness and sanctification, and redemption."

Now we are sure He is our righteousness, because God made Him to be.

If language means anything, we have a legal right now to stand in the Father's presence just as though sin had never been.

II Cor. 9:10 is now clear. "And he that supplieth seed to the sower and bread for food, shall supply and multiply your seed for sowing, and increase the fruits of your righteousness."

Jesus said, "I am the vine, and ye are the branches."

The vine is righteous and the branch is the righteousness of the vine.

So the fruits that the vine would naturally bear through the branches, will be called the fruits of righteousness.

Those fruits will be the same type of fruit that Jesus bore in His earth walk.

We have the joy of bearing a type of fruit that Jesus could not bear in His earth walk.

He could heal the sick, feed the hungry and raise the dead.

We bear another kind of fruit.

We lead men to Christ, which gives them eternal life.

We can lead men into the depths of the knowledge of God's righteousness that He wrought in Christ for them.

We can do things for men's spirits that Christ could not do.

You see, He had not yet died and paid the penalty for our sins, making the new creation possible.

We can have this spiritual fruitage in Christ.

This being established in righteousness gives us a foundation on which to stand and a reliance in our outlook on life.

You see, man has always been a servant of the Devil, a cringing slave.

This new creation, with this righteousness, makes him a master.

He is no longer a subject of the adversary.

He is now a master.

He does not talk of his weaknesses and failures, but rejoices in his new found ability to make the heart of the Father glad.

Now he is to act as though he knew he was righteous.

He is to take advantage of the fact that he is the righteousness of God.

He has a standing invitation to come into the Throne Room and visit with the Father at any time.

Hebrews 4:16. "Come boldly unto the throne of grace."

He knows he is the righteousness of God, just as clearly as that young woman knows she is married to her husband after the ceremony is performed.

She holds the place of wife in their home.

The two have become one.

This new creation knows that he is the righteousness of God, and that he has the legal right to the use of the Name of Jesus.

He knows the Name has all authority in three worlds.

By his union with Christ, he has become not only an heir to the authority in that Name, but he has become a present holder of that authority.

He may use it now.

When Jesus said, "All authority has been given unto me in heaven and on earth," that authority was for the New Creation, not for Himself.

This righteousness makes a man actually one with Christ.

It has given to man a creative ability, a dominating spirit.

He is an overcomer.

He is a master.

The new love life of the Master has taken possession of him.

He has become an actual Jesus man.

He takes Jesus' place on earth.

He is not like the men under the Old Covenant.

They had limited righteousness.

He possesses unlimited righteousness.

They had righteousness reckoned to them.

This righteousness is imparted to him; it is the very nature of the Father.

Israel became righteous by edict.

We have become righteous by the New Creation.

This new wonderful righteousness makes us fit companions of Jesus, and will fit us for our eternal fellowship with the Father through the ages.

This is really the genius of Redemption.

The miracle of the New Creation.

Now dare to think of yourself as being exactly what the Father says you are.

Dare to go into the Father's presence with fearless joy, making your request known to Him.

You see, He is your Father, you are His child.

In the Name of the Redeemer, you have access to the Father's presence at any time.

"Whatsoever ye ask in my Name, I shall give it you."

We are not honoring our place as sons, or our standing in righteousness unless we take our place.

Let us make the Father, the Lord Jesus and the Holy Spirit proud of us.

A Heart Message

When Jesus approached the tomb of Lazarus and said, "Roll away the stone." Martha must have clutched His arm and whispered, "It is too late Master, his body decayeth."

Jesus turned and looked into her face saying, "Martha, said I not unto thee, if thou believed, thou should see the glory of God."

The stone had been rolled away.

He stepped to the mouth of the tomb with divine assurance.

He had no sense of faith, or lack of it.

He illustrated unconscious righteousness.

He revealed what righteousness really is.

I have gone back in my dream life and stood by the side of the Master when He shouted, "Lazarus, come forth!"

My heart trembled and I whispered, "Master, why did you speak so loudly?"

You see I feared that Lazarus would not come forth.

I feared for the reputation of the Master.

What would the people think if He did not come forth?

These fearful thoughts, born of sense knowledge, were disrupted, for righteousness had spoken and Lazarus came forth.

The Incarnation was the union of Deity and humanity in the Babe of Bethlehem.

It was Love's intrusion into the realm of selfishness.

The long anticipated had at last arrived.

God was united with humanity.

The intrusion was not with an army . . . it was in the form of a dainty Babe.

It was like love, a helpless thing.

They called His Name Jesus.

That Name has filled the ages with songs and melodies.

It has brought courage to the defeated; liberty to the slave; strength to the weak; healing to the sick; and Eternal Life to the world.

That Babe who gave Mary her first great joy in that little town of Bethlehem, restored to woman the crown that she lost in the Garden of Eden.

She was man's help-meet, she became his slave after the Fall.

Jesus gave her hope, equality, and made her the queen of the heart of the New Creation.

Chapter III

THE INCARNATION

HE supernatural birth of the Child Jesus was part of the Covenant promise that God was keeping with Abraham. How could a child be born and not have the Adamic curse upon it?

How could a child be born without sin, so that he could stand in the presence of God without guilt or inferiority?

That is the miracle of the Incarnation.

Physiologists have proven beyond a question that the mother does not impart her blood to the babe that is formed.

Let me quote from "The Chemistry of the Blood" by M. R. De Haan, M.D., pages 31 and 32: "It is now definitely known that the blood which flows in an unborn babe's arteries and veins is not derived from the mother but is produced within the body of the foetus itself only after the introduction of the male sperm. An unfertilized ovum can never develop blood since the female egg does not by itself contain the elements essential for the production of the blood. It is only after the male element has entered the ovum that blood can develop.... The male element has added life to the egg.... Since there is no life in the egg until the male sperm unites with it, and the life is in the blood, it follows that the male sperm is the source of the blood."

If a fertile hen's egg is put in an incubator for several days, tiny veins of blood will form inside; that is not true of an egg that is not fertile.

This proves that the blood comes from the sperm of the male.

We know that if Jesus had been born of natural generation, fathered by Joseph, He would have had the blood of fallen man.

But He was conceived of the Holy Spirit, the life that was imparted to Him was from God.

The blood, which was the life of His body, came from the Most High Who overshadowed Mary.

The blood of that Babe was not the blood of a common man.

It did not have the taint of Sin.

We have come to know that sin is in the blood, and the human blood and the human spirit are in some way united.

Jesus had in Him the blood of God, His Father, just as every child has the blood of his or her father.

Life is in the blood.

Lev. 17:11: "For the life of the flesh is in the blood; and I have given it to you upon the altar to make atonement for your souls; for it is the blood that maketh atonement by reason of the life." (Am. Rev.)

Notice in the margin, "For the soul of the flesh is in the blood," again, "By reason of the life in the blood," or "by reason of the soul in the blood."

This is a very remarkable statement.

The life of the flesh is in the blood. When the blood is drawn out of the body, death follows.

The life of God was imparted in the blood of Jesus; thus Jesus was born without the Adamic nature, or the sin that came through Adam's blood in His conception.

Jesus was sinless.

You see, it is very evident that the life that is imparted to a man in the new birth enters his blood stream.

A scientist has just discovered that he can tell if a man has Eternal Life by his blood

When we became partakers of the Divine Nature, our spirits are recreated. There is a union in some way of spirit and blood, how we do not know. Thus our blood stream is cleansed of the sin that has come down through the blood of the human race.

Jesus was conceived without sin. His body was not mortal.

His body did not become mortal until the Father laid our sin nature upon Him when He hung on the cross.

The moment that He became sin, His body became mortal, only then could He die.

When this happened, spiritual death, the nature of Satan, took possession of His Spirit.

II Cor. 5:21: "Him who knew no sin he made to be sin on our behalf: that we might become the righteousness of God in him."

This phase of the Incarnation is of vital importance to us.

We can understand now why Jesus had dominion over the laws of nature, over the fish of the sea, over life and death. He healed the sick, raised the dead, He dominated the forces of darkness.

You see Jesus was the Covenant God manifested in the flesh, so it was necessary that He be circumcised into that Covenant.

He had once given that Covenant Law, and everything pertaining to it, to Moses through an angel.

Now He had come to fulfill His Covenant with Abraham.

The High Priesthood and the Senate had Jehovah on their hands, but they knew it not.

I have always wondered why they hated Him so. I understand their bitterness now. They had Satan's nature in them.

Satan hated Jesus, because He was God.

Consequently he tried to destroy Him from the time of His birth.

If we knew the history of the life of Jesus, it is likely that we would find that Satan made many attempts on His life.

Now you can understand the natural hatred that the Jews have for Him today.

He was their Blood Covenant God.

In their wild frenzy, born of Satanic power over them, they engineered His death.

There was bred into them a hatred that has come down through the ages.

They despise the very Name of Jesus.

They cannot help themselves. Jesus was their Blood Covenant God, manifested in the flesh.

The Legal Side

A legal Substitution would be impossible without an incarnation.

Deity must assume the liability of the Fall of humanity.

God must have known that man would Fall when He created him.

Man was created in the face of that fact.

Universal humanity has demanded that Deity assume the liability for that Fall.

A Substitute must be provided, actually taking man's place, suffering what humanity should suffer, meeting every claim of Justice in behalf of Fallen man.

Only then could God be vindicated.

An angel could not fulfill these demands.

No man could be the Substitute.

Only God Himself could fulfill these requirements.

An Incarnation of Deity and humanity was demanded.

The account of the Incarnation is found in the Gospel of Luke.

It tells of the Most High overshadowing the Virgin Mary, and she conceived in her womb that Holy Thing.

You see, Jesus did not partake of the mother's nature, she simply clothed Him with sinless flesh.

Had He been conceived of the seed of Joseph, His body would have been mortal.

Because He was conceived of the Holy Spirit, He possessed a body such as Adam had in the Garden before the Fall.

The Incarnation proves the pre-existence of the Man Jesus.

Phil. 2:6: "Who, existing in the form of God counted not the being on an equality with God a thing to be grasped, but emptied himself taking the form of a servant, being made in the likeness of men. And being found in fashion as a man, he humbled himself becoming obedient even unto death, yea the death of the cross."

Jn. 1:1: "In the beginning was the Word and the Word was with God, and the Word was God. The same was in the beginning with God. All things were made through him and without him was not anything made that was made."

There could not have been an Incarnation had not Jesus had a pre-existence as Deity.

In the English it is "Word"; in the Greek it is "Logos".

"In the beginning was the Logos, and the Logos was with God and the Logos was God.

There could be no Incarnation unless there was a perfect unity of Deity and humanity.

This occurred in the Man Jesus.

In the eyes of Sense Knowledge men it is a miracle.

In the eyes of God's Knowledge it is normal.

God's Knowledge is Spiritual; man's knowledge is of the Senses.

I Cor. 2:14: "For the natural man receiveth not the things of the Spirit, for they are foolishness unto him, and he cannot know them, for they are spiritually revealed."

I told you the Incarnation was the desire of Natural Man.

All primitive people have believed in an Incarnation.

To me, the Incarnation was God breaking into the Sense Realm, manifesting Himself in the flesh.

He made a Covenant with Abraham, now He is keeping that Covenant.

God actually thrust Himself upon the Jewish Nation, and especially upon the High Priesthood.

They did not realize that the God to Whom they had been offering sacrifices was at last among them.

He had come into their midst incognito.

He only revealed Himself to them through His miracles and intense love for humanity.

They could not recognize Him.

Satan had blinded the eyes of Israel, their Jehovah was among them, yet they did not know Him.

(Read the "Father and His Family" for a more complete discussion of this subject.)

Only a visitor from Heaven could tell you what the earth walk of the Man of Galilee meant to men.

Jehovah, of the Old Covenant made with Abraham, had suddenly appeared in the form of a Man.

Everybody thought that they knew Him as the son of Joseph and Mary.

He was the unknown.

He came unto those who were His own and they failed to penetrate through Love's disguise.

He went about doing Love deeds in Love's way.

He had a herald, John the Baptist, who pointed to Him and said, "Behold the Lamb of God who taketh away the sin of the world."

No one knew that John was heralding "The King of the Jews," their Jehovah who had come to His own people Israel.

As one reads the four Gospels he is convinced of a restraint upon each writer.

All of them knew who this Jesus was.

Luke had found Christ through Paul's ministry.

He knew the Pauline Revelation, but there is not one sentence in the writings of Luke that intimates this fact.

Mark had been Paul's companion and the same thing is true in his writings.

They only wrote what the Spirit gave them.

In John's Gospel there are but two suggestions of the Pauline Revelation, and yet John must have known that Revelation.

It thrills one when you think of the Divine restraint that was put upon every one of these men, who were to tell the story of The Man.

Chapter IV

WHAT HAPPENED DURING HIS EARTH WALK

HE visitation of Jehovah to His Covenant People can not be compared to any previous happenings in Israel's history as a nation, for it was unlike anything that they had ever known.

He was their Covenant God.

He had cut that solemn Covenant with Abraham.

There is no doubt in my mind but what the Master was ever conscious of this Covenant.

Jehovah had taken human form.

Not once did He reveal that He was the one who delivered their fathers out of Egypt.

They honored Moses more than they did Jehovah.

They worshipped the law more than they did Jehovah.

John 8:58-59: When Jesus said "Before Abraham was born, I am." They took up stones to cast at Him.

He startled them.

He had come very near to declaring who He really was, but Sense Knowledge men could not grasp it.

Matt. 22:31-32: "But as touching the resurrection of the dead, have ye not read that which was spoken unto you by God, saying, I am the God of Abraham, and the God of Isaac, and the God of Jacob? God is not the God of the dead but of the living."

This is the limit to which the Master could reveal Himself.

We, as believers, can look back upon that scene and recognize Him as the God of the Old Covenant, but we have Revelation Knowledge given to us through the Pauline Revelation.

Phil 2:5-9 gives you a graphic picture of Jesus in His earth walk. "Have this mind in you which was also in Christ Jesus: who, existing in the form of God, counted not the being on an equality with God a thing to be grasped, but emptied himself, taking the form of a servant, being made in the likeness of men; and being found in fashion as a man, he humbled himself, becoming obedient even unto death, yea, the death of the cross."

That is the earth walk of Jehovah.

I Tim. 3:16: "He who was manifested in the flesh."

II Cor. 4:4 shows the condition of Israel. "In whom the god of this world hath blinded the minds of the unbelieving, that the light of the gospel of the glory of Christ, who is the image of God, should not dawn upon them."

They were in spiritual darkness, which means Satanic bondage of the mind and spirit.

Gal. 4:4 will add to the picture. "But when the fullness of the time came, God sent forth his Son, born of a woman, born under the law, that we might receive the adoption of sons."

I have often wondered what would have happened if Israel's eyes had suddenly been opened.

Rejected

Is. 53:3: "He was despised, and rejected of men; a man of sorrows, and acquainted with grief: and as one from whom men hide their face he was despised; and we esteemed him not."

Jehovah had come to His own, but they despised Him.

He came to a place of suffering and rejection.

Lu. 18:31-34: "And he took unto him the twelve, and said unto them, Behold, we go up to Jerusalem, and all the things that are written through the prophets shall be accomplished unto the Son of man. For he shall be delivered up unto the Gentiles, and shall be mocked, and shamefully treated, and spit upon: and they shall scourge and kill him: and the third day he shall rise again."

The earth walk of Jehovah was the saddest walk ever taken.

We can remember in Matt. 27:22-26 where the priests were forcing Pilate to crucify Jesus and Pilate refused to be responsible for the blood of Jesus and washed his hands of the whole thing.

The mob cried "Let his blood be upon us and upon our children."

"Away with Him, away with Him." was their crazed demand.

They were crying for the blood of the God of Abraham and did not know it.

It is the Eternal God of the three tenses on trial by His own Blood Covenant people.

Heb. 13:8: "Jesus Christ, the same yesterday, today, and forever."

I Cor. 2:8 brings tears to the eyes. "Which none of the rulers of this world hath known: for had they known it, they would not have crucified the Lord of glory:"

They crucified the Lord of glory, and had no consciousness of the enormity of what they had done.

Paul was the first to receive a revelation of it.

He recognized Jesus as the Messiah, the God of the Old Covenant.

The God of the Old Covenant was this God of Love.

When He was manifested in the flesh as Jesus, it was really Love in human form.

Jesus had love's ability to bless and help men.

He knew who He was, why He came and what it would cost Him.

He was love incarnate.

"He came to seek and to save that which was lost."

He was the Son, whom God gave because He so loved these sin cursed deluded men.

In Luke 20:9-19 Jesus tells the story of the man who planted a vineyard and let it out to a husbandman, and went into another country for a long time. Then he sent a servant to visit the vineyard and receive fruit from it. But he was beaten and sent away empty-handed. This occurred three times and then the man decided to send his own son in the hope that they would reverence him. But the wicked husbandmen schemed to kill him, that the inheritance might be theirs.

God sent His Son to the vineyard and He was mistreated and crucified.

How little He was appreciated by His own.

God so loved.

It was Love that drove Jesus to become incarnate.

Love drove Him during His three and a half years of public ministry.

It was not the cruel spikes driven through His hands and feet by the Roman soldiers that held Him to the accursed cross; it was love.

John 6:37-38 might help us to grasp this more clearly. "All that which the Father giveth me shall come unto me; and him that cometh unto me, I shall in no wise cast out. For I am come down from heaven, not to do mine own will, but the will of Him that sent me."

John 1:4: "In him was life, and the life was the light of men."

John 10:10: "I came that they may have life, and may have it abundantly."

Love sent Him. Love sustained Him. Love was His ability.

He came with a single purpose, to redeem man from the realm of selfishness, where Satan ruled as king.

Jesus lived in this realm for thirty-three and one-half years.

He walked in the realm of selfishness and sin, and yet He walked in love.

Sin did not taint Him.

He was a stranger among His own people.

He was not understood by His mother, half-brothers or friends.

Love had come into Satan's realm.

He was love; He revealed love; He acted love.

He is the wonderful Jesus lover.

He was Satan's first Master.

How it thrills us, that Love should master Satan.

It makes us realize that love can master selfishness.

Jesus was the world's first free man.

No man had ever been free before Him.

What a thrilling statement, "If the Son shall make you free you shall be free in reality." (John 8:36)

Only a free man can set others free.

Only a lover can inspire others to love.

He was the first man free from selfishness that the world had ever known. No wonder they wanted to rid themselves of Him.

He did not seek His own.

He claimed nothing.

He gave everything.

He revealed a new kind of love.

He was love's first experience in human form.

He was God's Word made flesh.

Now you can understand, "In the beginning was the Word and the Word was with God, and the Word was God. All things were made through Him, and without Him was not anything made that was made."

He was the true knowledge, the Living Word.

Reason cannot understand this, but our Spirit feeds upon it with joy.

"The Word was made flesh and dwelt among us, and we beheld his glory as of the only begotten of the Father, full of grace and truth."

I wonder if you have ever noticed Moffat's translation of Heb. 4:12 "The Logos of God is a living thing, active and more cutting than any sword with double edge, penetrating to the very division of soul, spirit, joint and marrow. Scrutinizing the very thoughts and concepts of the heart. And no created thing is hidden from him, all things lie open and exposed before the eyes of him with whom we have to reckon."

He is referring to the Bible as we call it.

It is this Living Logos of God with whom we have to reckon.

The Word takes on personality.

The Word scrutinizes my thoughts.

The Word knows the innermost thoughts and conceptions of my heart.

This Word becomes a living thing on the lips of faith, and in the heart of love.

His actions were motivated by love

He did not try to prove His Deity by performing miracles, it was love that drove Him.

He wanted to alleviate suffering, agony, pain and grief.

Matt. 23:37 is one of the most vivid love pictures in the life of the Master. "O Jerusalem, Jerusalem, that killeth the prophets and stoneth them that art sent unto her! How often would I have gathered thy children together even as a hen gathereth her chickens under her wings, and ye would not!"

There is a sob in that. Tears mingled with agony.

One can hardly read the next verse.

"Behold your house is left unto you desolate."

Now you can understand those tragic words on the cross. "It is finished."

And then the veil of the temple was rent from top to bottom.

The Temple and the Holy of Holies were left desolate.

God had deserted it.

The Blood Covenant people had rejected their Jehovah and He was weeping over it.

He turned His steps toward the cross, the climax of His earth walk.

Jehovah, the Man of Galilee was born in a manger and reared among the poor and the under privileged.

"The foxes have holes, the birds of the air have nests, but the son of man has nowhere to lay his head."

It is hard to conceive the loneliness experienced by the Creator. Homes were closed against Him.

Rather than endure persecution and ridicule from the religious leaders of the day, they excluded their Jehovah from their circles.

He was an outcast.

"I was as a child cast upon thee from my mother's womb."

Satan sought His life from His birth.

Perhaps if we knew more about the earth walk of the Master, we would see a life filled with loneliness and heartaches.

"He is a man of sorrows and acquainted with grief."

He is the despised and the rejected one; and yet He is love.

Here is a picture of the God man. The One who had been driven by love to face the sacrifice of Himself.

Here is a demonstration of supreme love.

"God so loved that He gave."

The Son so loved that He suffered.

I believe He suffered more in the Garden than He did on the cross, for He was facing Hades.

On the Cross He felt the agony of Hades.

In the Garden He knew He must be made Sin, and His whole being shrank from it.

But His love drove Him on.

If you had followed Him into the Garden and heard Him pray, you would have been gripped by a strange New Force. It was Deity in agony.

He was revealing Love's power; something that the world had never before experienced.

Love's ability to suffer; Love's ability to sacrifice; Love's ability to endure.

It was Love's consent to be made Sin, go to Hades to suffer the torments of the damned for unworthy man, when He cried, "Not my will but thine be done." or "Not my will but thine be carried through to completion."

≡ǁ

Chapter V

WHAT HAPPENED IN THE GARDEN

EITY was facing Substitution in the Garden.

The crisis had come.

Jesus and three of His disciples had gone down to the place where He oft resorted for prayer, under those old, gnarled olive trees.

They had seen Him in prayer many times, but this was different.

Telling them to wait, and watch, He went alone a few steps, and fell upon His face.

They heard His voice, but could not distinguish His words.

He was facing the fact of being made Sin.

His disciples did not know this.

It was not a theological, or a metaphysical substitution, but He was to actually become a Substitute for fallen man.

He was to become a partaker of man's physical body.

He had not yet partaken of his Sin or mortality.

Jesus was conceived of the Holy Spirit, born of the virgin, but not by natural generation.

His body was like Adam's body in the Garden, before he sinned; it was neither mortal, or immortal.

It was a perfect human body.

Adam's body became mortal the moment that he sinned in the Garden. As mortal, his body became subject to disease and death.

The body Jesus possessed was a perfect human body.

You remember in John 10:17-18, "Therefore doth the Father love me because I lay down my life that I may take it again. No one taketh it away from me, but I lay it down of myself. I have authority to lay it down; I have authority to take it again. This authority receive I of my Father."

You can see by this that no one could kill Jesus.

His body was not mortal.

It did not become mortal until He hung on the cross.

"Him who knew no sin God made to become sin."

Jesus became sin.

His spirit received that terrible thing that came to Adam in the Garden, separating man from God.

It does not seem possible that Jesus could become Sin.

He was as Holy as God is Holy.

Sin had never touched Him.

True, for many years, He had lived in the midst of Sin.

"Tempted in all points like as we are," but Sin had never become a part of Him.

Now He must become Sin, and be separated from His Father.

As man's Sin Substitute, He must go to the place where the man who rejects Him must go.

He must suffer there until the entire debt that humanity owed Justice had been met.

Jesus knew why He came out from the Father.

He knew why He came into the world.

He knew before He came what He would have to face.

He knew what He must suffer.

Now you can understand that cry of agony, Matthew 26:36-46 "Then cometh Jesus with them unto a place called Gethsemane, and saith unto the disciples, Sit ye here, while I go yonder and pray.

"And he took with him Peter and the two sons of Zebedee, and began to be sorrowful and sore troubled.

"Then saith he unto them, My soul is exceeding sorrowful, even unto death: abide ye here, and watch with me.

"And he went forward a little, and fell on his face, and prayed, saying, My Father, if it be possible, let this cup pass away from me: nevertheless, not as I will, but as thou wilt.

"And he cometh unto the disciples and findeth them sleeping, and saith unto Peter, What, could ye not watch with me one hour?

"Watch and pray, that ye enter not into temptation: the spirit indeed is willing, but the flesh is weak.

"Again a second time he went away, and prayed, saying, My Father, if this cannot pass away except I drink it, thy will be done.

"And he came again and found them sleeping, for their eyes were heavy.

"And he left them again, and went away, and prayed a third time, saying again the same words.

"Then cometh he to the disciples, and saith unto them, Sleep on now, and take your rest: behold, the hour is at hand, and the Son of man is betrayed into the hands of sinners.

"Arise, let us be going: behold, he is at hand that betrayeth me.

Let us notice carefully; He said to the disciples, "My soul is exceedingly sorrowful even unto death: abide ye here, and watch with me." And then, falling on His face, He cried, "My Father, if it be possible, let this cup pass away from me: nevertheless, not as I will, but as thou wilt."

It is difficult for us to comprehend what this meant to the Master.

It was more than a separation from His Father, for three days and three nights.

He was to partake of Spiritual Death, the nature of the Adversary.

It has been said that God could not do a thing like that.

That is Sense Knowledge reasoning.

It is hard to understand how He could become Sin, but I know He did.

Sense Knowledge is limited, it cannot understand the Spiritual things of God.

In I Cor. 2:14 it says: "Now the natural man receiveth not the things of the Spirit of God: for they are foolishness unto him."

When one says to me, "You know, I cannot accept that, I cannot believe that, "I understand why.

You live in the Sense Realm just where Peter, James, and John lived when they walked with the Master.

Their minds were darkened as far as spiritual things were concerned.

They could not understand.

We have received the nature and the life of God.

We have the same Holy Spirit in us, who dwelt in Jesus, and raised Him from the dead.

That is the reason we understand the things of the Spirit.

Jesus knew that the moment had come, and He was to be made Sin.

He must partake of that dread nature of the Adversary.

His body would become mortal.

Satan would become His master.

This was the tragedy of the Garden. Jesus was to suffer the agonies of the lost.

He was to be reckoned among the transgressors.

He was to bear the diseases and sins of the human race.

He was to be forsaken by His Father.

It is no wonder that "He sweat, as it were, great drops of blood."

It is no wonder that He cried, "Father, if there is any other way—."

But there was no other way.

He, and He alone, must pay the penalty, or humanity would be eternally lost, and God, through eternity, would be childless.

Angels came and ministered to Him.

They did not minister to Him on the cross.

One of our literal translations reads, "If it be possible, take this cup from me; but not my will, but thine, be carried through to completion."

It was not a weak submission to the inevitable.

It was the Heroic Son of God facing humanity's great need and crying to the Father, "Carry this thing through to completion and save the human race."

That is why Paul cried, "He loved me, and gave himself up for me."

I have come to believe that there was deeper spiritual agony in the Garden than on the cross.

Anticipation of union with Spiritual Death was so hideous, so utterly unthinkable, that if angels had not ministered, we do not know what would have happened.

However, when Jesus came from the Garden and faced the sleeping disciples, He came as a Master.

He had won the fight.

He came not weeping, or bemoaning.

He came as the Conqueror!

There are two places in Christ's career that challenge the heart.

The first is, when He met Judas and the soldiers in the Garden.

Here He stands as the perfect Hero, the matchless Conqueror.

He had won the first battle.

Now He is ready for the trial, ready for the scourge, ready for the cross.

The second picture that thrills my heart is when He left the tomb and met the disciples, and cried, "All Hail!"

He had conquered.

He had put sin away.

He stands as the Lord of Lords now.

The shame and the agony of Hell are over.

He is the Hero God, my Lord, my Master, the Conqueror.

The battle in the Garden was spiritual.

Sense Knowledge cannot grasp it.

He had broken into the Sense Knowledge realm.

He had purposed to redeem man out of the hand of the Enemy.

To do it He must surrender Himself to that Enemy.

There are two great forces here, one seen, the other unseen, they are both dominated by Satan.

Satan ruled the Sanhedrin, the Senate, and the Roman governor.

He was seeking to dominate the Spirit of the Son of God and bring Him into subjection to himself.

Jesus knew the hour was coming when Satan would have Him under his control.

But now, facing the Soldiers and the trial of the Sanhedrin, and the judgment hall of Pilate, He walked as a King!

═ΙΙ═ΙΙ═ΙΙ═ΙΙ═ΙΙ═ΙΙ═ΙΙ═ΙΙ═ΙΙ═ΙΙ═ΙΙ═ΙΙ═ΙΙ═ΙΙ═ΙΙ═ΙΙ═ΙΙ═ΙΙ═ΙΙ═ΙΙ═ΙΙ═ΙΙ═ΙΙ

This is the tragedy of the Ages.

The One who had cut the Covenant with Abraham, cared for the children of Israel, like a nursing mother cares for her child, was on trial before the very High Priesthood that He had established.

He was not only Mary's Son but God, Jehovah Himself.

How vividly this scripture stands out, "He came unto His own and they that were His own received Him not."

They received Him to nail Him to the cross.

In that trial He stood before Pilate, the Senate, and the High Priesthood with the dignity of God. Not once did He call their attention to who He was.

He did not argue with them. He did not plead with them for mercy. "He had been delivered up by the determinate counsel and the foreknowledge of God."

The High Priesthood were the ones who were to carry out that determinate will of Love.

The Godhead was never shown so clearly as at the trial. He was every inch of Him, God.

He was not resigned; He was not submissive; He was not a martyr; He was love.

You remember how one glance from His eye broke Peter's heart.

No wonder Pontius Pilate sought to save Him from the cross.

Love was on trial—yes, but He was an absolute Master.

He was God manifested in the flesh.

═ΙΙ═ΙΙ═ΙΙ═ΙΙ═ΙΙ═ΙΙ═ΙΙ═ΙΙ═ΙΙ═ΙΙ═ΙΙ═ΙΙ═ΙΙ═ΙΙ═ΙΙ═ΙΙ═ΙΙ═ΙΙ═ΙΙ═ΙΙ═ΙΙ═ΙΙ═ΙΙ

Chapter VI

WHAT HAPPENED AT THE TRIAL

HE arrest and trial of Jesus is one of the tragedies of the human race, and especially of God's chosen people.

These Covenant people were familiar with the Abrahamic Covenant that had brought them into being as a Nation.

They knew the significance of the Blood Covenant.

The tragedy is that Jehovah, the Blood Covenant friend of Abraham, came to earth, conceived in the womb of the virgin Mary, born in a manger, welcomed by an angelic choir, grew up among His own people, yet remained a stranger to them.

They did not know Him.

They witnessed His miracles.

His compassion and love for them was recognized by all.

He turned water into wine, caused a tree to die by a single sentence, dominated the laws of nature, healed the sick, and raised the dead with words. His people witnessed all this.

He walked the waves and calmed the storm. Surely they must have known that He was the Son of God.

Jealousy had such a dominance over the hearts of the leaders that they sought to put Him to death.

He and His people could not live together.

You and I can see that He is Jehovah.

As a Nation they have Jehovah upon their hands.

What are they going to do with Him?

He had been circumcised into the Covenant.

He was a part of that Blood Covenant.

He had come to His own, yet they that were His own would have nothing to do with Him.

He came to redeem them, and they cast Him out.

He was the Jehovah of the Red Sea, and of Jericho.

He had caused the sun and moon to stand still in the days of Joshua.

He had blessed and protected them until they repudiated Him and were carried into captivity.

He was Jehovah, made manifest to the Senses as Jesus.

He tread the sod that He had given to Abraham for His Covenant people's home.

He was their Jehovah.

They were His Blood Covenant People.

He loved them.

They despised Him, and demanded His arrest.

They had their Jehovah on trial.

You, who understand the significance of the Blood Covenant, shudder at the thought of what they actually did.

The Person they had on trial, had cut the Covenant with Abraham.

Everyone of the men who shouted, "Crucify Him, Crucify Him," "Let His blood be upon us, and upon our children," had the mark of circumcision upon their flesh.

They were crying, "Crucify Abraham's Blood Covenant God."

I wonder if you have ever realized the tragedy of what they did?

What grief they brought upon themselves!

"Let His blood be upon us." Their Blood Covenant Jehovah.

They denied their Blood Covenant God.

They turned Him over to a heathen Governor to be scourged and crowned with thorns, and crucified.

His Covenant men followed Him up Calvary's Hill as He carried His Cross, hurling words of derision and hatred at Him.

Paul said, "Blindness had fallen upon them."

Their Covenant God was in their midst, and not a person recognized Him.

He was neither loved nor worshipped by His people.

Zech. 13:6 describes it vividly, "And one shall say unto him, "What are these wounds in thine hands? Then he shall answer, those with which I was wounded in the house of my friends." (Mar. Lovers)

He called them His Blood Covenant Lovers.

These same men insisted that their Jehovah be nailed to the cross.

This was the tragedy of the Ages.

I have often wondered why the Jewish people have suffered so intensely.

There seems to be born in them a bitter hatred toward the Man they had crucified. Man always hates the one he has betrayed.

They possess the same attitude today at the mention of His Name.

He was their Blood Covenant friend, and Lord.

He was betrayed in the House of Israel, His Blood Covenant friends.

His people treated Him as an enemy.

They crucified Him and shouted, "Let His blood be upon us."

It was Judgment Blood.

It should have been the Blood that would eternally bind them to their Covenant God, in the New Covenant.

They made it a Blood of Judgment, separating them from their Saviour and the Father God.

He came to make good the promises of the Covenant.

He came to make them Sons and Daughters.

He came to establish a New Covenant, with His own blood.

They crucified Him.

The cross was the climax of Love in manifestation.

There is no love without action.

It is not love until it acts.

Love was unveiled on the cross.

That God Man who hung there had come of His own volition.

He was not a martyr; He was a supreme Lover.

"God so loved." That God was Christ.

All of the attributes of God were made manifest on the cross.

There was a Holy dignity, a strange serenity, a marvelous sense of sureness in the entire scene.

Jesus was just as confident a master on the cross as He was when He said, "Roll away the stone."

Pilate and the Priesthood and the Senate did not sentence Jesus to death, nor did the Roman soldiers nail Him to the tree, it was the unseen forces of Satan that guided them. They were merely instruments.

That Potentate believed that he had gained the ascendancy and that he was the master. He did not know that he was destroying himself by attempting to destroy the man.

That Jewish hierarchy did not know that in the mind of Justice they were crucifying the Jewish nation, and that the high Priesthood would die with Christ on the cross.

They did not know that the sacrifice of bulls and goats was ended.

When Jesus said, "It is finished," their priesthood was finished.

Chapter VII

WHAT HAPPENED ON THE CROSS

ENSE knowledge stands mute in the presence of the tragedy of the eternities.

Deity is to suffer for humanity. "Justice had demanded and He becomes answerable." Justice has decreed that man must pay the penalty of his transgression.

Man is in bankruptcy.

Man is impotent, helpless.

Man is a slave.

He cannot approach God.

He cannot meet the demands of justice.

And so, out of the heart of God, comes the solution of the human problem. His Son says, "Here am I, send Me." And on towards the cross He goes.

One of the most difficult features of this study is the disciples' ignorance of what is taking place.

They did not know Jesus in His earth walk. They were but Sense Knowledge men.

By that I mean all the knowledge they had, had come to them through what they could see, what they could hear, what they could feel, what they could taste, or what they could smell. These five senses were their only teachers.

1 John 1:1-3. "That which was from the beginning, that which we have heard, that which we have seen with our eyes, that which we beheld and our hands handled, concerning the Word of life (and the life was manifested, and we have seen, and bear witness, and declare unto you the life, the eternal life, which was with the Father, and was manifested unto us).

'That which we have seen and heard declare we unto you also, that ye also may have fellowship with us: yea and our fellowship is with the Father and with His Son Jesus Christ."

Understand that our scholastic world has no other knowledge than that which has come through these five senses.

There is another kind of knowledge that the world folk repudiate.

It is the Revelation Knowledge, God's Knowledge.

The disciples did not know that Jesus was going to be made Sin on the cross.

They did not know that He was going to die Spiritually.

They did not know that He was their Substitute, and that He was going to put sin away and make it possible for them legally to receive Eternal Life, the very Nature of God.

They did not know that the Man of the cross was going to rise again from the dead, and was going to be the Head of a New Creation, a new type of man.

No one had ever told them about receiving Eternal Life.

No one had ever received Eternal Life before; it was a new experience, a revolutionary one.

They had listened to Jesus and heard Him say, "I am come that ye may have life and have it abundantly."

They had heard Him say, "He that believeth on Me shall pass out of death into Life."

They knew He used a strange word, "Zoe." They did not know there were two kinds of life, "Zoe" and "Psuche."

Nor did they know that there are two kinds of Death, Physical Death and Spiritual Death.

No one had ever told them that there was a New Kind of Life coming to the world, and every one who became a partaker of this Life would become a New Creation.

They did not know where Jesus had gone when His body was pronounced dead on the cross. They did not see the awful tragedy that was taking place when He hung there.

They witnessed the strange phenomenon mentioned in Luke 23:44. "It was now about the sixth hour and a darkness came over the whole land until the ninth hour."

Creation went into mourning when the Creator became man's substitute.

Matthew 27:51-54 says that an earthquake took place.

Creation was shaken to the very center by the tragedy of Deity becoming humanity's substitute.

Matthew 27:51 tells us, "And behold, the veil of the temple was rent in two from the top to the bottom."

No one knew what this meant.

The Holy of Holies was no longer the home of Jehovah. He had moved out of the temple.

Jesus had fulfilled the Abrahamic Covenant and the law of the Covenant.

There was no need of a priesthood any longer.

The high priest finished his ministry when he made the great sacrifice of the Lamb of God, who was to take away the sin of the world.

There will no longer be a Holy of Holies, a place for the atonement blood to be sprinkled.

When Jesus said, "I will destroy this temple and restore it in three days," how little they understood Him.

I Cor. 3:16, "Know ye not that ye are a temple of God and that the Spirit of God dwelleth in you?" The new creation is God's temple today.

His death and substitution will make the former temple unnecessary.

He is going to become the new High Priest.

"He had made one sacrifice for sins forever, and He is to sit down at the right hand of the Majesty on High."

The priests did not know that their priestly duties had ended.

The Jews that stood about the cross did not know what God was going to give to Paul twenty years later. Read the first eight chapters of Hebrews.

Gal. 2:20 in the Revised Version, reads: "I have been crucified with Christ." The whole Jewish nation had been crucified with Him.

The entire human race had been crucified with Him. They did not know it.

History tells us that 50 years after the crucifixion of Jesus, there was not one member of the high priestly family living; neither could they find a member of the Davidic family.

The priesthood was to last "until Shiloh came." Shiloh had come and they did not know Him.

Gen. 49:10. "The scepter shall not depart from Judah, nor a lawgiver from between his feet, until Shiloh come: And unto him shall the obedience of the peoples be."

They did not know that the Man hanging on the cross was their Shiloh.

They did not know that the priesthood would stop functioning before God, when they slew Him.

They did not know that the Mosaic law which they worshipped, but did not keep, would stop functioning when they nailed Him to the Cross.

Here are some facts for our hearts to assimilate.

Is. 53:4-6: "Surely he hath borne our sicknesses and carried our pains: and we have come to esteem him as the one who was stricken, smitten of God and afflicted, who was wounded for our transgressions, who was bruised for our iniquities. And the chastisement of our peace was upon him, and with his stripes we are healed. And we like sheep have gone astray, we have turned everyone to his own way; and Jehovah hath made to strike upon him the iniquity of us all." (Lit.)

Here is a picture of the Substitutionary Sacrifice of Christ.

In the ninth verse, Isaiah says, "He made his grave with the wicked and with the rich man in his death."

The word, "death," is plural in the Hebrew, indicating that Jesus died twice on the cross.

He died Spiritually the moment that God laid our Sin upon Him. The moment that "Him who knew no sin became sin," that precious body became mortal, and He could die physically.

If you will notice, the moment He became Sin, darkness came down over Golgotha, and He cried the bitter cry, "My God, my God, why hast thou forsaken me?"

That was the darkest hour of eternity in Heaven. How the angels must have covered their faces.

The universe went into mourning when God made Jesus Sin.

Now we can understand Isaiah 53:10-12 "Yet it pleased Jehovah to bruise him: he hath made him sick: and when thou shalt make his soul an offering for sin, he shall see his seed, he shall prolong his days, and the pleasure of Jehovah shall prosper in his hand. He shall see the travail of his soul and be satisfied. It was demanded and he became answerable on the ground of his sacrifice. God will be able to justify many because he bore their iniquities, because he poured out his soul unto death and was numbered with the transgressors and he bore the sins of many and now is able to make intercession for them." (That is almost a literal translation.)

The twenty-second Psalm gives a graphic picture of the crucifixion of Jesus. It is more vivid than that of John, Matthew, or Mark, who witnessed it.

That crucifixion scene was written a thousand years before the lone Galilean hung there on the cross.

It opens with His cry on the cross, "My God, my God, why hast thou forsaken me? Why are thou so far from helping me and from the words of my groaning? O my God, I cry in the day time, but thou answerest not, and in the night season I am not silent. But thou art holy, O thou that inhabitest the praises of Israel. Our fathers trusted in thee. They trusted and thou dost deliver them. They cried unto thee and were delivered. They trusted in thee and were not put to shame. But I am a worm and no man: a reproach of men, and despised of the people."

This is a monologue.

You can see Him hanging there on the cross. He is paying no attention to the mob about Him. The deep physical agony, the awful shame of hanging naked in the presence of His enemies, the knowledge that His Father had forsaken Him is breaking His heart.

He remembers Israel's history. Jehovah had heard their cry and delivered them.

But He says the strangest words, "But thou art holy." What does that mean?

He is becoming sin.

Can you hear those parched lips cry, "I am a worm and no man."

He is spiritually dead. The worm.

He has become what John's Gospel, 3:14, said. "And as Moses lifted up the serpent in the wilderness, even so must the Son of Man be lifted up."

He had been lifted up as a serpent. Serpent is Satan.

Jesus knew He was going to be lifted up, united with the Adversary.

That holy man of God.

44

And the Psalmist sees Him as the worm, the reproach of the people. "All they that see me, laugh me to scorn: they shoot out the lip, they shake the head, saying, He trusted on Jehovah that he would deliver him: let us see him deliver him. (Marginal) Let him come down from the cross, and we will believe on him."

Now the monologue continues. He is hanging there surrounded by the multitude, led on by the high priest.

He cries, "But thou art he that took me out of the womb: thou didst make me trust when I was upon my mother's breasts. I was cast upon thee from the womb: thou art my God since my mother bore me."

You remember as soon as He was born, an angel told Joseph to take Him to Egypt. He was the God-cared-for baby of Bethlehem.

But now He is the God-forsaken Son of God, hanging upon the cross.

As the forsaken Man of Galilee, there He cries, "Be not far from Me; for trouble is near; for there is none to help."

The disciples are powerless. His own people, headed by the High Priest, have seen that He was nailed to the cross. "There is none to help."

And now He says the strangest words, "Many bulls have compassed me: strong bulls of Bashan have beset me round about. They gape upon me with their mouth, as a ravening and roaring lion."

What does He mean by the "Bulls of Bashan." It is the Sanhedrin and the Senate. They are the leaders of the herd, they gape upon Him, and they crucify Him.

Then comes the strange sentence, "I am poured out like water. All my bones are out of joint: my heart melteth within me.

What does it mean?

John 19:31-35 tells us what happened. "The Jews therefore, because it was the Preparation, that the bodies should not remain upon the cross upon the sabbath (for the day of that sabbath was a high day), asked of Pilate that their legs might be broken and that they might be taken away. The soldiers therefore came, and brake the legs of the first, and of the other that was crucified with him: but when they came to Jesus, and saw he was dead already, they brake not his legs: howbeit one of the soldiers with a spear pierced his side, and straightway there came out blood and water."

Jesus had died of a ruptured heart.

When that happened, His blood from all parts of the body poured in through that rent, into the sack that holds the heart.

Then as the body cooled, the red corpuscles coagulated and rose to the top. The white serum settled to the bottom.

When that Roman soldier's spear pierced the sack that held the blood, water poured out first. Then the coagulated blood oozed out, rolled down His side onto the ground, and John bore witness of it.

The Psalmist, a thousand years before that dread scene on Golgotha, described it more accurately than any of the eye- witnesses.

Hear the next sentences. "My strength is dried up like a potsherd; and my tongue cleaveth to my jaws; and thou hast brought me into the dust of death."

That is the reason they always gave the crucified one a drink of vinegar.

Then comes the next awful sentence. "For dogs have compassed me: a company of evil-doers have inclosed me: they pierce my hands and my feet."

Who were these dogs? The Roman soldiers. They had nailed Him to the cross. And you notice He called them dogs. Jews always called people outside of the covenant "dogs," a "no-people."

"I may count all my bones." Every bone in His body was crying out against this inhuman, devilish agony.

But to me one of the saddest sentences that dropped from those parched lips was, "They look, they stare upon me." That Holy Man hangs naked before His enemies.

"They look, they stare upon me. They part my garments among them, and upon my vesture do they cast lots."

> Under the shadow of the cross,
> Seated upon the ground,
> Gambling for His undervest,
> The soldiers pressed around.
>
> They heeded not His agony,
> The death sweat or the pain.
> They were like our modern folk;
> Their hearts were set on gain.

You have seen a picture written 250 years before crucifixion was practiced, a thousand years before the tragedy of Golgotha was enacted.

But do not let the physical sufferings or the graphic scene of Golgotha rob you of the reality of the Son of God being made Sin for us.

We have seen that Jesus' death on the cross was more than a physical death.

He was there by Divine choice and plan.

He actually was made Sin with our Sin.

He was God's Substitute for the human race.

When He was made Sin, He was turned over by God to the Adversary.

When that heart-breaking sentence fell from His lips, "My God, my God, why hast thou forsaken me?" Satan became His master.

You remember that He uttered the sentence, "It is finished."

You can now understand that He did not mean that He had finished His Substitutionary work, but that He had finished the work the Father gave Him to do first.

As a Son, He had done His Father's will, spoken His Father's word, and done His Father's works.

Second, He had finished His work as the son of Abraham. He had fulfilled the Abrahamic Covenant.

He had kept the Mosaic Law.

Now He is to become a Substitute and deal with the Sin Problem.

He is to put Sin away.

He is to satisfy the claims of Justice against the human race.

He could not do that in His physical life.

Sin basically is a spiritual thing, so it must be dealt with in the spirit realm.

If Jesus paid the penalty of Sin on the cross, then Sin is but a physical act.

If His death paid it, then every man could die for himself.

Sin is in the spirit realm.

His physical death was but a means to an end.

Paul says in Heb. 10:12 "But he, when he had offered one sacrifice for sins forever, sat down at the right hand of God."

When Jesus died, His spirit was taken by the Adversary, and carried to the place where the sinner's spirit goes when he dies.

The rending of the veil was the rending of the Abrahamic Covenant.

How little these people knew when they cried, "Let his blood be upon us and upon our children," they were asking that the blood of love become a blood of judgment.

They did not know they slew themselves on that cross.

Annas and Caiaphas were slaying the Lamb of God, their last sacrifice before Jehovah.

They will slay animals before men, but it will not be accepted by God.

There will be no atonement for Israel, nor covering for their sins.

There is a redemption awaiting them, but their eyes are blinded.

They have crucified the Jehovah who cut the Covenant with Abraham, but they are ignorant of it.

He was Jehovah manifested in the flesh and there was not an eye that penetrated through the disguise.

When He cried, "It is finished," it was the end of the Abrahamic Covenant.

As far as the earth walk of that people, it was the ringing down of the curtain upon the Jewish nation.

Chapter VIII

WHAT HAPPENED WHEN THE VEIL WAS RENT

HERE were many fateful things that happened while Jesus hung upon the cross, but I want you to think about two of the events that contain eternal significance.

You remember that Jesus said, "Matthew 23:38, "Behold, your house is left unto you desolate."

Jesus was uttering a prediction of the most marvelous event that ever happened to the Israelite people.

Again, Matthew 26:61, "But afterward came two, and said, This man said, I am able to destroy the temple of God, and to build it in three days."

Jesus was standing before the Sanhedrin. The High Priesthood and the elders at last had Him on their hands, and they were bringing witnesses against Him.

Two of them accused Him of saying, "I am able to destroy the temple and build it in three days."

Little did they realize what Jesus was referring to, or that it would actually take place.

The Temple was destroyed as the place where Jehovah dwelt, when the veil was rent from top to bottom.

In Matthew 27:50-51, "Jesus cried again with a loud voice, and yielded up his spirit. And behold, the veil of the temple was rent in two from the top to the bottom."

Just before that happened, He uttered those three strange words, "It is finished."

What did He mean?

First, I want you to notice the statement, "It is finished."

He had come as the Incarnate One, the God Man, Jehovah!

He had walked before His Father for thirty-three and one-half years.

Twice, He had heard His Father say, "This is my beloved Son in whom I am well pleased."

There had never been a man before who had pleased the Father.

I call Him the Father-pleaser.

Every other man had lived to please himself.

At last God has a man on earth that lives to do His will.

You remember these four remarkable scriptures.

John 4:32-34, "But he said unto them, I have meat to eat that ye know not. The disciples therefore said one to another, Hath any man brought him aught to eat? Jesus saith unto them, My meat is to do the will of him that sent me, and to accomplish his work."

John 5:30 "I can of myself do nothing: as I hear, I judge: and my

49

judgment is righteous; because I seek not mine own will, but the will of him that sent me."

Notice, "I seek not my own will, but the will of Him who sent me."

Again Jesus said, John 6:38 "For I am come down from heaven, not to do mine own will, but the will of him that sent me."

The reason He came was to do the will of His Father.

He died for our sins because it was the will of the Father.

But John 8:29 is to me, in some ways, the sweetest. "He that sent me is with me; he hath not left me alone; for I do always the things that are pleasing to him."

How precious Jesus must have been to the Father.

How precious one is who lives that Jesus life, to Him who gave Jesus for us.

Jesus lived to please and make glad the heart of Him, who created the first man in the Garden, who became humanity's failure.

Next, Jesus not only satisfied the heart of the Father, but He had been circumcised into the Abrahamic Covenant. He had become a part of Israel. He was Abraham's Blood Covenant friend, Jehovah!

Now He must fulfill that Abrahamic Covenant.

What would that mean to Israel? That Covenant had given them their national life, had given them their Law, their Sacrifice, their Priesthood.

It had given them their national home.

It had given them the Atonement Blood.

It had given them their Temple where God dwelt in the Holy of Holies.

It had given them their Messiah whom they had nailed to the cross. Jehovah manifested in the flesh!

And when Jesus said, "It is finished," the Abrahamic Covenant had come to an end, so far as Israel was concerned.

Not only was the Covenant at an end, but everything connected with the Covenant.

It was the end of the Covenant Law, the Ten Commandments.

They had worshipped that Law. It was a law of death; a law that begat fear in the hearts of men.

It was not a law of love, nor a law of life.

Paul called it, "the law of sin and of death," but they loved it.

It was a law for natural man, just as the Abrahamic Covenant was a Covenant for natural man.

There will never be another scape-goat to bear Israel's sins away in type.

It was the end of the Holy of Holies in Israel's Temple.

This is what it meant, when Jesus said, "It is finished," and yielded up His spirit, "the curtain was rent from top to bottom," and their Temple was left desolate.

It was no wonder that there was an earthquake.

It is no wonder that darkness came down and settled over Jerusalem and Golgotha.

The heart of the Son of Man had been broken on that cross.

He had been made Sin.

He had said, "It is finished," and all Heaven heard it.

The ears of man had not taken it in.

I wonder if you realize that it was not only the end of Israel, and of Judah, and all that pertained to them as a nation; but it was the beginning of a new Covenant.

You remember that Jesus said, just before He died, Luke 22:14-23 "with desire I have desired to eat this passover with you before I suffer: for I say unto you, I shall not eat it, until it be fulfilled in the kingdom of God."

It is the story of the institution of the Lord's Supper.

Notice the language. "He took bread, and when he had given thanks, he brake it, and gave to them saying, This is my body which is given for you: this do in remembrance of me."

Of the cup He said, "This cup is the New Covenant, in my blood, even that which is poured out for you."

In Matthew 26:28 "This is my blood of the covenant, which is poured out for many unto remission of sins."

The Old Covenant died.

The New Covenant is born.

The New Covenant began functioning on the Day of Pentecost.

It was not established in Heaven until Jesus carried His blood into the Holy of Holies and poured it out there as the red seal upon the document of our redemption.

How little we have appreciated the New Covenant in His blood.

Old Covenant men had a limited righteousness, and on the ground of that, they performed the miracles and prodigies that the Israel people saw.

We hear the marvelous prayer of Abraham, in Genesis 18.

The miracles that happened under Moses' ministry in leading Israel out of Egypt.

The miracles of Joshua, of Elijah and Elisha, of David and Daniel, were performed with limited righteousness.

It was based upon a Covenant sealed with the blood of Abraham, along with the blood of God's offering, a bullock.

Now we have a New Covenant, and it is sealed not with the blood of bulls and goats, but the united blood of Deity and humanity.

The strange feature about that offering was that the representatives of the Abrahamic Covenant offered Jesus, their Jehovah, on the cross altar and did not know it.

He was forced onto the hands of the Roman government to be

crucified.

So the hands of the Priesthood and the hands of the Roman Gentiles met on the sacrifice that they offered upon the altar of the cross.

Israel became identified with the offering.

The Gentile world became identified with that offering.

Just as no offering was acceptable unless hands had been laid on its head under the Abrahamic Covenant, so the offering up of the body of Christ was made acceptable because the priesthood and the Roman government laid their hands upon our beloved Lord, "The Lamb of God who was to take away the sin of the world."

This new Covenant gave to us the beginning of the New Creation, the Circumcision of the heart.

Colossians 2:11-12; "In whom ye were also circumcised with a circumcision not made with hands, in the putting off of the body of the flesh (or rule of the senses) in the circumcision of Christ; having been buried with him in baptism, where in ye were also raised with him through faith in the working of God, who raised him from the dead."

A person entered the Abrahamic Covenant by circumcision.

We enter the New Covenant by circumcision of the heart, or the New Birth.

The First Covenant was made for Natural Man. Everything connected with it was for Natural man.

The New Covenant is for the recreated man, the New Man in Christ.

It is not only the beginning of a New Creation, but it is the beginning of a new Priesthood.

Hebrews 8:1-2, "Now in the things which we are saying the chief point is this: We have such a high priest, who sat down on the right hand of the throne of the Majesty in the heavens, a minister of the sanctuary, and of the true tabernacle, which the Lord pitched, not man."

You should read very carefully Hebrews 8:1-13.

We haven't space to copy it all, but it tells of the New Covenant that is to be given to the New Creation. It closes with this significant sentence, "A new covenant, he hath made the first old. But that which is becoming old and waxeth aged is nigh unto vanishing away."

There was an annulling of the foregoing Commandment and foregoing Covenant, and foregoing Priesthood and Sacrifices.

There was the inauguration of the New Covenant, the New Priesthood with the New Creation folk who are called a New Covenant people.

The New Covenant had a New Law, John 13:34-35: "A New commandment I give unto you, that ye love one another; even as I have loved you, that ye also love one another. By this shall all men

52

know that ye are my disciples, if ye have love one to another."

The Old Covenant had a law of fear.

The New Covenant has a Law of Life and a Law of Love.

Paul tells us in Romans 8:1-2: "There is therefore now no condemnation to them that are in Christ Jesus. For the law of the Spirit of life in Christ Jesus made me free from the law of sin and of death."

Notice the contrast between the two Covenants, the Old Covenant with Natural man and the New Covenant with the recreated man.

Our hearts cannot too clearly grasp the significance of the fact that this New Covenant Law of Love is to govern the Church absolutely.

Leviticus and Deuteronomy are an exposition of the Law of the Old Covenant, known as the Ten Commandments.

The Pauline Revelation is an exposition of the New Covenant Law.

I Corinthians 13 gives us in condensed form the outstanding features of this New Covenant Law.

Hebrews 9:11-12 gives us a description of Christ's entering the Heavenly Holy of Holies, with His blood.

Note carefully this translation: "Nor yet with the blood of goats and calves but with His own blood, entered in once for all into the Holy place, having obtained eternal redemption."

The high priest entered with blood once a year to cover the broken law for Spiritually Dead Israel.

But Christ enters with His blood into the Heavenly Holy of Holies once for all, obtaining for us an Eternal Redemption.

How it thrills the heart that our Redemption is Eternal.

The fourteenth verse is so suggestive. "How much more shall the blood of Christ, who through the eternal Spirit offered himself without blemish unto God, cleanse your conscience (or spirit) from dead works to serve the living God?"

"For this cause He is the Mediator of a New Covenant."

He died for the sins under the First Covenant.

You must not omit Hebrews 9:24: "For Christ entered not into a holy place made with hands, like in pattern to the true; but into heaven itself, now to appear before the face of God for us."

I Peter 2:3-10 gives us a picture of the new sacrifices that we are to offer to the Father.

Here is a view of the two-fold Priesthood of the Church.

From 3 to 5 we see the Holy Priesthood offering up " . . . spiritual sacrifices acceptable to God through Jesus Christ."

This is the private Holy of Holies of the individual believer.

Hebrews 13:15 gives a beautiful picture of it. "Through him then let us offer up a sacrifice of praise to God continually, that is, the fruit of lips which make confession to his name."

In the Holy Priesthood we offer up our praises, our worship, and our love, through Jesus Christ, our Lord.

That ties perfectly with Ephesians 5:20: "Giving thanks always for all things in the name of our Lord Jesus Christ to God, even the Father."

We never offer up thanksgiving to the Father but through the Name of Jesus.

Why? Oh, that glorifies the Son. It constantly stresses upon our hearts His place of Mediation and of His great High-Priestly Ministry.

In the ninth and tenth verses, we catch a glimpse of the Royal Priesthood.

"But ye are an elect race, a royal priesthood, a holy nation, a people for God's own possession, that ye may show forth the excellencies of Him who called you out of darkness into his marvelous light; who in time past were no people, but now are the people of God, who had not obtained mercy, but now have obtained mercy."

Notice here is a wonder ministry.

It is toward the world, and also toward the Church.

Before the world it is the revealing of Christ as their Redeemer.

I stand before the congregation and I minister to them in the Royal Priesthood.

But the heart should always remember this.

My Royal Priesthood does not function in reality unless there has been time spent in the Holy Priesthood.

Unless my lips have been bearing fruit of love and worship and fellowship with the Father in the holy priesthood, they will be dead lips when I attempt to unfold the Word to the Body of Christ in the Royal Priesthood.

The Word becomes a living thing in the lips of love.

The lips of love are always faith-creating lips.

The words that you speak will be satiated with love and grace and tempered with wisdom.

Because we have taken our Bible, gone into the Holy Place and fellowshipped and visited with our Father until our whole being seems to be saturated with love.

Hebrews 10:19-22 gives us a glimpse of the new Holy of Holies.

"Having therefore, brethren, boldness to enter into the holy place by the blood of Jesus, by the way which he dedicated for us, a new and living way, through the veil, that is to say, his flesh; and having a great priest over the house of God; let us draw near with a true heart in fulness of faith, having our body washed with pure water." Our earth walk is cleansed by the Word.

In Hebrews 4:16, He has invited us to come with boldness unto the Throne of Grace.

That is the new Holy of Holies, the new Throne-room where we, as sons and daughters, have a standing invitation to come.

We not only come when our hearts are burdened with grief and need, but we come when our hearts are filled with joy and laughter.

We come when our hearts are filled with gratitude and love and praise.

Our Father is holding a reception all the time for us.

We go in there and make our requests known. We open our hearts to Him with the fullest confidence.

We have Jesus' assurance, "Whatsoever ye shall ask of the Father in my name, He will give it to you."

We are His love children.

Now we come to one of the most remarkable sentences from the lips of Jesus.

We have already quoted it, but I want you to note it again.

It is Matthew 26:61 and I Cor. 3:16.

He told them that He could destroy that Temple and build it again in three days.

They did not understand it, but He did destroy the Temple, didn't He? When He said, "It is finished," the temple was an empty building and God was getting ready to move into the new building. The veil guarding the Holy of Holies was rent in twain from top to bottom; no Holy of Holies on earth now.

"Know ye not that ye are the temple of God and that the spirit of God dwelleth in you. If any man destroy the temple of God, him shall God destroy for the temple of God is holy, and such are ye."

That is the temple that Jesus raised or built in three days.

That is the new home of God.

Not only is the Church the corporate body in which He dwells, but I Cor. 6:19 shows us a closer contact and relationship.

"Know ye not that your body is the temple of the Holy Spirit which is in you, which ye have from God: And ye are not your own; for ye were bought with a price. Glorify God therefore in your body."

Notice that your body, as His Temple, is a holy thing.

Romans 12:1-2: "I beseech you therefore, brethern, by the mercies of God, to present your bodies a living sacrifice, holy acceptable to God, which is your spiritual service."

This body becomes God's Holy of Holies.

It is the most hallowed thing on earth today.

I can understand how Satan hates it and would fill it with disease and sickness.

I can understand how Jesus spent most of His three years of public ministry in healing sick bodies. He knew what they were to be. He knew what they would be when the spirit of the man in that body was recreated and received the nature and life of the Father. He knew that body would then become the earthly Holy of Holies in which God would dwell.

What a wonderful thing it is that we can have God in us!

"Greater is He that is in you than He that is in the world."

I wonder if Ephesians 2:19-22 has ever challenged your heart?

"So then ye are no more strangers and sojourners, but ye are fellow-citizens with the saints and of the household of God, being built upon the foundation of the apostles and prophets, Christ Jesus himself being the chief corner stone; in whom each several building, fitly framed together groweth into a holy temple in the Lord, in whom ye also are builded together for a habitation of God in the Spirit."

Notice that we are fitly framed together and we grow into a Holy Temple in the Lord and we become builded together for a habitation of God in the Spirit."

Now you can understand that strange phenomenon that takes place when a body of believers begin to walk in Love. The room where they gather is charged with something that men can feel. I have known the power of God to be so great in a congregation that men and women could feel it as they walked past the open door.

I have heard their strange confession, "There was some power that pulled me into the church that day."

That is when the Body of Christ becomes the habitation of the Spirit, when love is let loose in us.

The very atmosphere of God dominates us.

In Colossians 1:18, Jesus is called the Head of the Church, and as the Head of the Body, the Church, He is the beginning or first-born from the dead.

You remember that He tasted death (spiritual death) on the cross. The moment that sin was laid upon His spirit, He died in spirit.

I showed you in another part of the book that He died in spirit first, then in body.

He was made alive twice.

"He was made alive in spirit." 1 Pet. 3:18.

Then His body was raised from the dead.

He was the first person ever Born Again.

Those on the Day of Pentecost were the first group ever Born Again.

What a wonder thing it is to become a partaker of the Divine Nature!

To become the very Sons and Daughters of God!

Just to capitulate a bit, the Old Covenant was not for Gentiles, but for Israel alone.

No Gentile could get into that Covenant except through a long process.

It was for Natural man only, not for Christians.

That Old Covenant has been fulfilled and laid aside.

How unhappy it is that men and women are trying to get into that Covenant now.

We have large bodies of men and women today who are attempting to keep the Mosaic law, as they call it, but it has been fulfilled and laid aside.

Note this fact; no one could keep that Covenant outside of Palestine.

They could not keep it without a High Priest and Sacrifices and Blood Atonement.

The Israelite who had left his homeland for commercial reasons was obliged to come back once a year in order to keep under the Abrahamic Covenant blood sacrifice.

How unfortunate it is that men try to get under that Covenant today and try to keep the Law, when God has set it aside and everything that pertains to it.

The New Covenant has its Priesthood, Sacrifices and its Holy of Holies.

But it has a Redemption instead of Atonement.

It has Remission instead of a Scape-goat.

It has a New Birth instead of circumcision.

It has fellowship with the Father in the place of the burnt offering, the peace offering and the meal offering.

It has the name of Jesus instead of Urim and Thummin.

The New Covenant has the Lord's table in the place of the Passover.

We are sons instead of servants.

We have the law of love in the place of the law of sin and of death.

We have life in the place of death.

We have righteousness instead of condemnation.

When we break the law of love, we have an Advocate.

They have judgment and stoning and death.

We have a living Father who watches over us.

This chapter is a revelation of eternal love.

It is Jesus, the master of Satan, yielded to his dread control.

It is God manifest in the flesh being made sin.

He has uttered that heart-breaking cry, "My God, my God, why hast thou forsaken me?"

He is humanity's substitute, paying the penalty of its transgressions.

He is bearing the fruit of Adam's sin in the substitution.

He is suffering the torments of the damned, for the men who crucified Him.

He was God manifest in the flesh as He walked the earth; He is God made sin now, suffering in our stead.

If one could write over this entire chapter in letters of living light, one word, it would be "Love."

"God so loved."

Our language is inadequate to express this love of One who became sin for us.

Deity is paying the penalty for having loved humanity so much, and for craving a family.

He is suffering because He created humanity; because He brought man into being.

"Him who knew no sin has become sin."

"He is putting sin away by the sacrifice of himself."

The agonies of Deity in redeeming the human race can never be known by finite mind.

Chapter IX

WHAT HAPPENED DURING THE THREE DAYS
AND THREE NIGHTS

HE nature of the substitute's suffering has been a challenge down through the centuries.

What was the nature of His suffering?

Was it mental, physical, or in some inexplicable way, spiritual?

It could not have been mental, because He and the Father planned it.

It could not be physical, because sin is not a physical thing.

A man can think murder, but he has to speak or act before he becomes answerable to the law.

You see, man deals only in the sense knowledge realm.

God deals in the spiritual realm.

In the first sermon preached after the resurrection of the Lord, Peter says these remarkable words, "Him, being delivered up by the determinate counsel and foreknowledge of God, ye by the hand of lawless men did crucify and slay: whom God raised up, having loosed the pangs of death: because it was not possible that he should be holden of it." Acts 2:23-24.

A better rendering of the words, "pangs of death" is the "birth-throes of death," suggesting that the church was born out of the birth-throes of the spirit of Jesus.

Read the twenty-seventh verse: "Because thou wilt not leave my soul unto (in) Hades, neither wilt thou give thy Holy One to see corruption." (In Joseph's tomb)

Also verses 29-31. "Brethren, I may say unto you freely of the patriarch David, that he both died and was buried, and his tomb is with us unto this day."

"Being therefore a prophet, and knowing that God had sworn with an oath to him, that of the fruit of his loins he would set one upon his throne; he foreseeing this spake of the resurrection of Christ, that neither was left unto (in) Hades, nor did his flesh see corruption."

Peter gave a striking message. He spoke by revelation.

He told them that Jesus was then seated at the right hand of God, yet no intimation had been given in regard to it.

Notice this fact, "His soul was not left in Hades, nor did His body see corruption in Joseph's tomb.

The eighty-eighth Psalm gives us a foreview of the substitutionary sacrifice of Jesus in Hades. For a more extended exposition of this, read the chapter on "How God Can Be Just" in my book, *"The Father and his Family."*

I want you to notice this now, Jesus was actually delivered up on account of our trespasses, and He was raised when He had satisfied the claims of justice.

There are two or three objections that we might consider.

You remember Jesus said to the thief on the cross, "Today, thou shalt be with me in Paradise."

You understand there is no punctuation in the Greek.

Punctuation is determined by the emphasis.

Rotherham, in his notes on this, makes it read, "I say unto you Today," (the word today is emphatic, and in our American Revision it is capitalized.)

It should read like this: "I say unto you Today, thou shalt be with me in Paradise."

Just as you might say, "I say unto you today, I will meet you in Portland."

This does not mean that Jesus went to Paradise when the spirit left His body.

Paradise was a place for the Old Testament saints to await the completion of the redemptive work of Christ. They were waiting for the fulfillment of the First Covenant.

In other words, to put it in modern parlance, they were waiting for Him to cash the promissory notes of the Atonement blood for the fifteen hundred years.

But this work was not finished on the cross.

It was not finished until Jesus arose from the dead and carried His blood into the Holy of Holies, and the supreme court of the universe had accepted that blood and had justified the Old Testament saints.

Now you can understand Romans 4:25. "He was delivered up for our trespasses, and was raised when we, as Jews and Gentiles, were justified." (Lit.)

You understand that there can be no substitution unless Christ actually paid the spiritual penalty of man's transgression.

Adam's sin gave Satan dominion over him.

Satan breathed into Adam his own nature. Adam was actually born again in the Garden.

He did not have God's nature.

He had perfect human nature.

He had perfect human life.

Into his spirit, Satan now poured his own nature.

Man instantly became a liar, a cringing, cowardly being.

That nature has been reproduced in the human race down through the ages.

John 8:44-45 gives us a perfect picture of what happened to the human race through Adam's transgression.

"Ye are of your father the devil, and the lusts of your father it is your will to do. He was a murderer from the beginning, and standeth not in the truth, because there is no truth in him. When he speaketh a lie, he speaketh of his own: for he is a liar, and the father thereof. But because I say the truth, ye believe me not."

The word truth means reality.

Satan is the absence of reality.

That explains Romans 1:25. Speaking of universal man, he said, "For they exchanged the reality of God for the unreal." This translation is striking, but it is true to the original.

You can see now the condition that man is in.

He has lost his approach to God.

He has no standing with God.

He has no covenant claims on God.

He has become, as Paul tells us in Romans 8:7, "Because the mind of the flesh is enmity against God; for it is not subject to the law of God, neither indeed can it be."

His very nature is antagonistic toward God.

That explains why, in that great substitution that God wrought in His son, He had to make provision on legal grounds for man to become a partaker of His own nature, eternal life.

Isaiah 53 is a picture of the substitute suffering in our stead.

It is neither mental nor physical suffering.

It is suffering in the spirit.

Psalms 22 gives us a picture of His physical suffering, but this scripture in Isaiah gives us a picture of His spirit, as the body of the Son of God hung upon the cross.

"He was despised and rejected of men, a man of pains and acquainted with sickness. Surely he hath born our sicknesses and carried our pains, and we have come to esteem him as the one who was stricken, smitten of God, and afflicted (with our diseases.") (Lit.)

It is an unhappy thing that we are so slow in coming to appreciate what He actually did on our behalf.

Now mark you this thing, God looks upon disease as a spiritual thing.

He did not lay our physical diseases upon the spirit of Christ, but our spiritual diseases.

Then disease is a spiritual fact, just as sin is a spiritual fact.

It was God who laid our diseases upon Him.

"He was wounded for our transgressions. He was bruised for our iniquities, and the chastisement of our peace was upon him, and with his stripes we are healed. All we like sheep have gone astray, we have turned every one to his own way; and Jehovah hath laid on him the iniquity of us all." Isaiah 53:5-6.

The thoughtful student will notice the fact; that He dealt with the disease problem before He dealt with the sin problem.

It is not for us to ask why He did that, but the fact remains that He did.

It may be that we are so conscious of our senses that it was necessary that God deal with the sense man before He dealt with the spiritual man.

We should notice this fact, that man is in the same class with God.

He is an eternal being.

He is a spirit being.

He was so created that he could become a partaker of God's nature.

He was wounded in His spirit with our iniquities.

The chastisement that could bring peace to us was upon Him, and "by his stripes we are healed."

They are not physical stripes.

It is justice dealing with our substitute, in the spirit realm.

Our American Revision reads: "Yet it pleased Jehovah to bruise him; he hath put him to grief: when thou shalt make his soul an offering for sin, he shall see his seed, he shall prolong his days, and the pleasure of Jehovah shall prosper in his hand. He shall see the travail of his soul, and shall be satisfied; by the knowledge of himself shall my righteous servant justify many; and he shall bear their iniquities. Therefore will I divide him a portion with the great, and he shall divide the spoil with the strong; because he poured out his soul unto death, and was numbered with the transgressors; yet he bare the sin of many, and made intercession for the transgressors."

Another translation for the tenth verse reads: "Yet it pleased Jehovah to bruise him and to make him sick. He was filled with grief and sickness."

Another: "He was covered with disease as from a plague."

"Through burden of sickness."

"Hash laid on him weakness."

There is no escaping this fact that disease and sin are one.

They have one common origin.

They have two different ways of manifesting themselves, one in the physical body, the other in the spiritual.

Romans 8:3 declares, "That God has condemned sin in the flesh." No doubt, by that he means sin and diseases, for they have a common origin in Satan and are under condemnation by God.

But I think the most dreadful statement in this chapter is: "When thou shalt make his soul an offering for sin," or "thou shalt make his life a sin offering."

But notice this translation: "Though his soul take on itself guilt."

The eleventh verse has some striking translations.

After He had justified Him in spirit, "then he was begotten of God."

I Tim. 3:16: "He was justified in spirit."

He is the first born out of spiritual death, the first person who was ever born again.

Now our hearts can take in this truth. "Through the travail of his soul shall he see light in fulness, and by his knowledge shall my servant bring justice to me, and of their guilt shall he bear the burden." (Isaiah 53:11.)

That translation is striking.

The Variant Reading: "He shall satisfy hunger and thirst with the travail of his soul."

From these translations, you can catch a glimpse of the substitutionary sacrifice of our great Master.

His spirit absolutely became impregnated with the sin nature of the world.

He sank to the lowest depths of Hades, according to the eighty-eighth Psalm.

The human mind cannot grasp it.

There is no language that will describe it.

We have nothing by which we can compare it.

"Him who knew no sin, God made to become sin."

The sin offering under the law, had sin reckoned to them.

Christ did not have sin reckoned to Him.

He was made to be sin.

The Israelites had righteousness reckoned to them.

We have righteousness imparted to us.

This righteousness enables us to stand in the Father's presence as though sin had never been.

Just two or three striking translations from the eighty-eighth Psalm.

"My soul is full of troubles, satiated with evils.

"My soul has arrived at Sheol, the kingdom of death. I am become a man without God."

The sixth verse: "In the lowest pit, the pit of the dense darkness."

Seventh: "Thou dost lay thy wrath fully upon me." "All thy breakers thou hast poured upon me." "Thou hast let all thy waves strike upon me." "Thou hast let come all thy breakers upon me."

Ninth: "I am wasted away."

In the fifteenth verse, we catch a sentence that hurts. "I am distracted, I am brought low; I have born thy terrors so that I am distracted. Thy streams of wrath have cut me off, destroyed me."

This gives us a picture of something beyond human reason; that our princely Saviour suffered on our behalf, that He might make us righteous.

Righteousness, you understand, means the ability to stand in the Father's presence without the sense of guilt, condemnation or inferiority.

We stand there as sons in the presence of the Father of love.

We have been recreated out of His own heart.

We are of His own substance.

You know it will be a great day when large bodies of believers come to understand what they really are in Christ.

"Wherefore if any man is in Christ, he is a new creation."

He is a new species; something the world had never known until the Day of Pentecost.

He is so nearly like Christ, so utterly one with Him, that Christ can say, "I am the vine, and ye are the branches."

We are become partakers of His own nature. Not only that, but He has deigned to come and make His home in our bodies.

I cannot grasp this with sense knowledge.

I simply know that it is a fact, and my spirit bears witness with the Word that it is true.

He is in me now. That great, mighty Spirit who raised Jesus from the dead is in me as I dictate this.

He is illuminating the Word, causing my heart to grasp the wonders of the Father's grace as unveiled in Jesus.

Can't you see the vital need of our studying to find out what we really are in Christ? What the spirit, through the Word, has really wrought in us that has made us acceptable to Him until He can whisper, "You are in the Beloved."

That means you are as near the Father's heart as Jesus is.

Jesus' great prayer in John 17 almost clamors in this request, "Father that they may know that thou lovest them, even as thou lovest me."

I Timothy 3:16: After God had "justified him in spirit." And then made Him "alive in spirit." I Peter 3:18: "Because Christ also suffered for sins once, the righteous for the unrighteous, that he might bring us to God; being put to death in the flesh, but made alive in the spirit."

This is a remarkable fact, that Jesus was born again before He was raised from the dead.

Acts 13:29-34: "And when they had fulfilled all things that were written of him, they took him down from the tree, and laid him in a tomb. But God raised him from the dead: and he was seen for many days of them that came up with him from Galilee to Jerusalem, who are now his witnesses unto the people. And we bring you good tidings of the promise made unto the fathers, that God hath fulfilled the same unto our children, in that he raised up Jesus; as also it is written in the second psalm, Thou art my Son, this day have I begotten thee. And as concerning that he raised him up from the dead, now no more to return to corruption, he hath spoken on this wise, I will give you the holy and sure blessings of David."

One of the most dramatic and remarkable incidents in regard to Christ's substitutionary work takes place.

Colossians 2:15 gives a description of a battle that took place in Hades before Jesus arose from the dead.

In Luke, it tells us that He went into the strong man's house and bound him.

Jesus, after He had been justified and made alive in spirit, became Satan's master.

And "having despoiled the principalities and the powers, he made a show of them openly, triumphing over them in it." (Col. 2:15.)

It is more graphic in a marginal rendering.

"Having put off from himself the principalities and the powers, (It would seem as though the whole hosts of hell were upon him. He was going through agonies beyond words, and suddenly is justified, made alive.)

"He hurls back the hosts of darkness."

Hebrews 2:14: "He put to naught the hosts of darkness," or He let them be defeated; He paralyzed their death dealing power.

And when He met John, He said, "I am he that was dead and behold, I am alive forever more, and I have the keys of death and of Hades."

He had conquered Satan.

He had stripped him of his authority.

Keys represent authority.

Jesus was the master of all hell.

He did not conquer Satan for Himself.

Jesus conquered Satan for us, for you and for me.

It was as though you personally had met Satan and conquered him and stripped him of his authority and stood a master over him.

Now you can understand why Jesus gave us the power of attorney to use His Name.

He said, "In my name ye shall cast out demons. Ye shall lay hands on the sick and they shall recover."

Remember Matthew 28:18-19: "All authority hath been given unto me in heaven and on earth. Go ye therefore, and make students of the whole world." (Disciple means student.)

And these students have the authority that Jesus manifested in hell, today in that mighty Name.

If you could only realize this fact, that you actually have a legal right to the authority and power invested in Jesus' Name and you can use it.

You have the power of attorney to use Jesus' Name.

You are an absolute master of Satanic forces.

Now we are prepared to understand Romans 4:25, "Who was delivered up for our trespasses, and was raised for our justification."

If you had stood by the cross with Peter and John and the others, you would not have seen anything more than they saw. Not one of them knew that God was dealing with Christ's spirit, that He was "stricken, smitten of God and afflicted" with all the diseases and all the sins of the human.

The marginal readings in the cross-reference Bible of Isaiah 52:13-15 will throw much light on this problem.

Verses 14 and 15. "Just as many were dumbfounded at him, for deformed was his appearance so as not to be a man, and his figure so as not to be human."

Another translates it, "Just as many were amazed over him, and princes on his account shuddered."

Another translates: "His visage was so unlike to a man, and his form unlike to the forms of men."

Another: "So deformed was his appearance so as not to be a man, and his figure no more resembled man."

One cannot understand how the spirit of Jesus had been so deformed by the sins and the diseases of the human, that He no longer resembled a man.

Isaiah 53:5 has some striking translations. "A man of pains, of suffering, of sorrow, acquainted with grief, familiar with ailing (literal, sickness)."

The fourth verse is also striking. "Yet our diseases it was he who bore, and our sufferings. He bore the load while we thought him plague-struck, smitten of God and afflicted."

Another translation of this same verse: "Surely our ailments he bore, and our pains he did take for his burden; but we counted him stricken, smitten of God and degraded."

I want you to notice this Variant reading from the tenth to the twelfth verses.

Isaiah 53:11. "From the travail of his soul shall he see, by his knowledge be satisfied. My servant, the righteous, righteousness wins he for many, and their guilt he takes for his load." SMI; "Through the travail of his soul shall he see light in fulness (Lit. shall see light, shall be satiated); by his knowledge shall my servant bring justification to many, and of their guilt shall he bear the burden." WHI.

This translation is clearer: "Who was delivered up on account of our trespasses and was raised when we stand right, or justified, before God."

There are two phases of righteousness.

When Christ was raised from the tomb, everyone had righteousness set to their account, which would give them a legal right to eternal life, but this righteousness did not become theirs until they personally accepted Jesus Christ as their Saviour and confessed Him as their Lord.

Those who teach a universal salvation have only grasped the legal side of righteousness.

Every child in Israel had a legal right to all the benefits of the Covenant, but it did not become theirs personally until they were individually circumcised.

Eternal life becomes ours the moment we personally take Jesus Christ as Saviour and confess Him as the Lord of our Life.

We think of the climaxes in the brief life of the Man.

There was the one in the garden, the one at the trial and another at the cross, but only an angel could depict the climax of His resurrection.

The Man had paid the penalty of humanity's transgression.

He had been made sin.

He had been justified.

The Father had said to Him, "This day have I begotten thee," and He was made alive in spirit. "The first born from the dead."

He had thrown off the forces of darkness that had held Him in captivity.

He had stripped them of their authority and dominion over man.

He was the master of death and the conqueror of the grave.

He put on immortality as a garment, appearing among the disciples in the same simple godlike way in which He had mingled with them for three and one half years.

His lips uttered just two words, "All Hail!"

Redemption morn had come.

The New Creation could now become a reality.

The Son of God, who died like a lamb had arisen as the Lord High Priest of the New Covenant.

Love lingers over that new title.

The most sacred, the most beautiful that lips ever uttered, but as yet, unknown by man.

Mary fell at His feet and He said, "Touch me not for I have not yet ascended to my Father."

He entered into Heaven as the High Priest and carried His own blood into the new Holy of Holies.

Chapter X

WHAT HAPPENED AT THE RESURRECTION

HE resurrection of Jesus was the greatest event that ever took place, either in the sense realm or in the spirit realm. Satan is defeated.

The head of the New Creation is a victor.

He is the example for all members of the New Creation. They are to be overcomers, masters of circumstances and all demoniacal forces.

Christ arose to the full stature of His Godhead in the presence of the adversary.

He threw off from Himself the principalities and the powers.

He made a show of them in the presence of all Hell.

Then, taking the trophies from the hand of the conquered, He arose from the dead.

You can hear Him say, "I was dead, and behold I am alive forevermore, and I have the keys of death and of Hades." (Rev. 1:18)

That brings to your memory the scene in Matthew 28:5- 6. The women had come down to the sepulchre. They found it empty, but an angel was there.

"And the angel answered and said unto the women, Fear not ye; for I know that ye seek Jesus, who hath been crucified. He is not here; for he is risen, even as he said. Come, see the place where the Lord lay."

The Lord of sin, sickness, death and Satan.

He died as Jesus, the Lamb.

He arose as the Lord High Priest.

He conquered death and the grave.

When Mary met Him, she fell at His feet, calling Him her Lord. He said to her, "Touch me not, for I have not yet ascended to my Father."

His last cry on the cross had been, "My God, my God, why hast thou forsaken me?"

He had paid the penalty of man's transgression. He had met the demands of justice.

Now He is about to take His own blood, as the High Priest, into the Heavenly Holy of Holies, to make the eternal redemption.

The resurrection of the Lord Jesus let love loose.

It enabled God to give eternal life, a perfect redemption, a perfect freedom, to Satan-enslaved man.

It made Jesus the head of a new creation.

It made this new creation man a creative being, who is in the class with God.

Out of that dark tomb came the light of the ages.

Now we can understand John 8:12, "I am the light of the world. He that followeth me shall not walk in the darkness, but shall have the light of life."

New creation men, a new type of men, a new species of men, are to walk the earth.

There were physical giants upon the earth at one time.

Now there are spiritual giants.

There are sense knowledge giants.

Now with the Pauline revelation unveiled, we will have spiritual giants.

John 1:4 shines out with radiance now.

"In him was life; and the life was the light of men."

Jesus had the life and the light in Him, but it could not shine during His earth walk.

Now He is giving that life to the little light-bearers, the new creation. In the midst of this darkness of sense knowledge, we are to shine as lights.

The life of which Jesus spoke so often was going to produce the light, the wisdom, the creative ability, that the world had never had.

There had not been a creative mind since the fall of man.

It was life and light from the tomb.

It came streaming forth, a radiance that has lighted the world.

If one were poetically inclined, he would become lyrical thinking of that empty sepulchre as giving birth to life, light, freedom, love and a new creation.

They thought they had rid themselves of Jesus, but that empty sepulchre gave birth to millions of Jesus men.

When one realizes what the resurrection of Jesus has meant to the human race, one stands amazed.

The open sepulchre gave birth to woman's freedom. She was a slave, and is today wherever the resurrection of Jesus has not gained sway over the minds of men.

It gave to man a new kind of love.

The only kind of love which man has ever known grew out of selfishness.

Natural man has no real love; it is refined selfishness.

If the object of his love to whom he has written lyrics and poetry rejects this love and dares to love another, his love changes to hatred and murder.

There is no solution for the human problem outside of the resurrection of Christ. Romans 4:25. "Who was delivered up on the account of our trespasses, and was raised when we were justified."

The fratricidal wars that have swept the ages and now have engulfed the world, could never have occurred if this new kind of love that Jesus brought to the world had gained the mastery.

We talk about patriotism; it has often been the parent of slaughter.

When the Master arose from the tomb in Jerusalem, He gave to the world a new kind of love, a new kind of life, out of which has grown a new kind of ethics and a new standard of living that would destroy war, hatred, jealousy, bitterness and selfishness in every form.

Jesus lived it.

Paul gives it to us.

He says, "It seeketh not its own but always its brother's good."

This new thing that came out of the empty sepulchre is the most revolutionary thing that ever touched the human.

It never takes advantage.

It never does an unkind thing.

It is never the parent of tyranny or bloodshed.

It gives birth to new creation men with God's life.

Not only imparting His nature to men, but actually coming into them and making their body His temple.

This new kind of life gives to man the ability to stand in the presence of God without the sense of guilt, condemnation or inferiority.

It took out of man the fear of circumstances, the dread of old age, the shrinking of the weak in the presence of the strong.

It made all men equal.

It made the strong bear the burdens of the weak.

It made the world a safe place for babies to be born and reared.

A strange day has dawned.

It was the matchless day of the new creation.

It was the wonder day when Jesus was born in the manger back yonder, but it was a greater day when God made provision for the new creation.

From the resurrection morn to Pentecost, those forty or fifty days were filled with God's plans for the birth of the church.

The resurrection morn was the morn of all morns!

It was the beginning of a new day when a new kind of love should dominate where hatred had run riot.

The resurrection of Jesus meant Satan was defeated; his slaves would become his masters.

Every new creation would be a conqueror.

His new sense of righteousness gave him dominance where fear had held sway.

Fearless mastery of the old slave-driver has taken possession.

The New Creation is a master.

"Who is he that overcometh the world? He that is born of God." (1 John 5:4-5.)

71

If mystery can fascinate, then these forty days are fascinating.

To my knowledge, there has been but one book written on this theme, yet most momentous things take place during this period.

After His resurrection, He carried His blood into the Holy of Holies; for you remember He died a lamb and He arose the High Priest of the New Covenant.

That New Covenant had just come into being when He carried His blood into the presence of the supreme court of the universe.

The blood was accepted.

That blood cleansed the Old Testament saints who had trusted in the blood of bulls and goats; it put their sin away.

That blood sealed the New Covenant.

It only required one offering.

Jesus was then enabled to go to Paradise and proclaim to the awaiting saints of the Old Covenant that He had made a perfect redemption, He had cashed every one of the promissory notes of Atonement.

Now the Old Testament saints are ready to go into Heaven.

"In my Father's house are many dwelling places."

They are to go and occupy their new home.

Among them will be everyone who trusted in the promise from Adam to the thief on the cross.

Chapter XI.

WHAT HAPPENED DURING THE FORTY DAYS

HESE are wonder days of obscurity to the average person, but by carefully going over the four gospels, then back through Paul's epistles, we have caught glimpses here and there of what transpired during those forty days.

A scripture with which we are becoming familiar, will be our first one. Hebrews 9:12, "Nor yet with the blood of goats and calves, but with his own blood, entered in once for all into the holy place, having obtained eternal redemption." (Lit.)

The Spirit is telling, through Paul, of Jesus as the New High Priest carrying His blood into the Holy of Holies and making eternal redemption, but before He goes in with His blood, there is a little human touch to the drama that we must not overlook.

It is in John 20:11-18. The Master appeared, to Mary, the sister of Martha. She did not know that it was He.

He said unto her so tenderly, "Woman, why weepest thou? Whom seekest thou?"

She thought He was the gardener.

One can hardly keep the tears from filling the eyes when reading how she said, "Sir, if thou hast born him hence, tell me where thou hast laid him, and I will take him away."

Jesus wept over the tomb of Lazarus. You know, I am thinking that He wept again at this place.

How deeply His heart must have been touched by her loyalty, and He turned to her and said one word, "Mary."

It was the old voice, the voice that they had come to love. How many times He had said, "Mary," in their home in Bethany. How many times she had heard Him say, "Martha," and "Lazarus."

It broke over her like a flood. She turned, looked at Him, fell at His feet and whispered, "Raboni."

She would have clasped His feet, and I do not wonder. How many times I have said, "Oh, if I could kiss those feet and the wounds in those beautiful hands."

But He said unto her so tenderly, just above a whisper, "Touch me not, I am not yet ascended to my Father."

You know what He meant.

He died a lamb; He died a substitute.

He arose as the Lord High Priest.

You remember the curtain was rent in the Holy of Holies from top to bottom. That meant there was no longer a high priest under the Old Covenant. The priesthood was done away.

There was no Law; it had been fulfilled.

No more sacrifices; the High Priest did not know it, but he had offered the lamb of God as the great sacrifice for eternity.

And the sacrificial lamb had risen from the dead as the High Priest of the New Covenant.

The Abrahamic Covenant was completed.

There is a new High Priest now, who did not belong to the family of Levi, but one who had been made a High Priest with all authority.

He is after the order of Melchizedek. He is outside of the priesthood family.

And so He says tenderly to Mary, "Touch me not, I have not yet ascended to my Father."

He says in effect, "I am going to take my blood in to the New Holy of Holies, sprinkle it on the mercy seat just as our High Priests have been doing once a year, but mine is going to be an eternal sacrifice. I am going to consummate your redemption, Mary. You do not know it, daughter, but I died for your sins, I have put them away.

"Now I am carrying the seal of your sacrifice unto my Father.

"When I come back, you can put your hands on me, you can touch me, you may know that I am flesh and blood, but now goodbye. I am going to my Father."

And He was gone.

We have allowed our hearts to romance just a bit here, but it was all a part of the dream, the plan.

You see it in the book of Hebrews.

After Jesus had done this wonder thing of carrying His blood into the Heavenly Holy of Holies, and the supreme court of the universe had accepted it, He had other things to do.

You see, He died for the sins under the first Covenant.

Hebrews 9:15. "And for this cause he is the mediator of a New Covenant, that a death having taken place for the redemption of the transgressions that were under the First Covenant, they that have been called may receive the promise of the eternal inheritance."

Notice in this, that the New Covenant began to function the moment that He carried His blood into the Heavenly Holy of Holies and that He instantly became the Mediator between fallen man and the Father.

He had died for the redemption of transgressions under the first Covenant. Now these Old Covenant men are to receive their eternal inheritance.

They were promised it every time the High Priest carried blood into the Holy of Holies.

That was a promissory note, and had gone on for fifteen hundred years. Now Jesus cashed these notes. The Old Testament Fathers were redeemed. They were in Paradise waiting for Him

The thief that died on the cross was among them in Paradise Jesus was going to keep His promise now.

He said, "I say unto you today, thou shalt be with me in Paradise." He did not say He was going to Paradise with him, but He told him that day, that He would be with him in Paradise.

Now He is keeping His promise.

Peter throws some light on this in I Peter 3:18-19, "Because Christ also suffered for sins once, the righteous for the unrighteous, that he might bring us to God; being put to death in the flesh, but made alive in his spirit; in which also he went and preached unto the spirits in prison."

You see, Jesus did not have anything to preach to them until His blood had been carried into the Holy of Holies.

It tells in Ephesians 4:8-9, "Wherefore he saith, when he ascended on high, he led captivity captive, And gave gifts unto men." (Now this, He ascended, what is it but that he also descended into the lower parts of the earth?)

What does he mean by this? He went into the place where the Old Testament saints were kept in Paradise and proclaimed to them the joyful news of their redemption and He took these captives captive and He gave unto them gifts.

And notice in Acts I, that a cloud received Him when He went up.

Acts 1:9-11. "And when he had said these things, as they were looking, he was taken up; and a cloud received him out of their sight. And while they were looking steadfastly into Heaven as he went, behold, two men stood by them in white apparel, who also said, Ye men of Galilee, why stand ye looking into heaven? this Jesus who was received up from you into heaven, shall so come in like manner as ye behold him going into heaven."

I do not know whether or not you noticed it, but in so many places a cloud played a large part. For instance, in the transfiguration, while He is speaking, a bright cloud overshadowed them, and a voice out of the cloud spoke to them,—At the coming back of the Master, the Son of Man shall come in the clouds of Heaven.

And now a cloud received Him.

Most of our spiritual commentators believe that the cloud was the Old Testament saints taken up from Paradise into Heaven.

I agree with them.

It is a beautiful conception that they have given to us of the Master taking these Old Testament saints like Abraham, David and others as the first-fruits of His great sacrifice.

No one on earth had yet received the benefit of His substitutionary sacrifice. No one had yet been born again. No one knew anything about it.

It is doubtful if even the most intimate knew what those forty days meant, and that their loved ones had gone to meet God.

There was another beautiful thing that happened during the

75

forty days. It was the trip to Emmaus. Luke 24:13-35.

We cannot spare the space in the book to quote it, but I would like to have you read it.

Two of the disciples were on their way to this little town.

They were talking about the thing that had happened, and the reports that had filled Jerusalem of the resurrection of Jesus. A stranger joined them and asked them what they were talking about.

Cleopas answered, "Dost thou alone sojourn in Jerusalem and not know the things which are come to pass there in these days?"

Then He asked them what things they meant.

They said, "The things concerning Jesus the Nazarene, who was a prophet mighty in deed and word before God and all the people; and how the chief priests and our rulers delivered him up to be condemned to death, and crucified him."

They said, "And certain of them that were with us went to the tomb, and found it even so as the women had said: but him they saw not."

Then Jesus said, "O foolish men, and slow of heart to believe in all that the prophets have spoken!"

You see they were still natural men; He was but a prophet to them.

They could not understand the scripture, and I imagine that after they had received the Holy Spirit, that walk to Emmaus became one of the most thrilling testimonies in that little group in Jerusalem.

Another thing happened in Luke 24:44-46. "Then opened he their minds, that they might understand the scriptures."

He never had to open their minds again after the Day of Pentecost, for they had then received eternal life, and could understand spiritual things.

John 20:22-23 is evidently the same meeting that is recorded in Luke 24:44-46. Now He breathes on them and says, "Receive ye the Holy Spirit."

This is not receiving the Holy Spirit as on the Day of Pentecost.

This was not receiving eternal life.

This was simply giving them inspiration to understand what He was teaching.

None of the disciples had yet received eternal life.

The Spirit had not yet come to take up His ministry of the New Covenant.

Understand clearly the Old Covenant had passed with the rent veil. The New Covenant had come into being with Jesus' blood being carried into the Holy of Holies.

But the ministry of the Holy Spirit was held up for ten days after Jesus had left them.

You see the Master had to sit down at the right hand of the

Majesty on High and enter into His rest.

Then the Holy Spirit took up His ministry. He came on the Day of Pentecost which was fifty days after the crucifixion.

The disciples were waiting in the Upper Room.

They were not acting very wisely. They were attempting to put somebody in Judas' place, and they were doing it by natural man's method.

They were casting their lots like men today, flip up a penny and say, "Heads or tails."

The Father ignored them altogether.

When the time came that He was ready, He appointed Saul of Tarsus in the place of Judas.

You notice in Acts 1:14, it says "These all with one accord continued steadfastly in prayer, with the women, and Mary the mother of Jesus, and with his brethren."

We must not carry over from Paul's epistles anything to this scene.

I want you to clearly understand that up to this time nobody had been born again.

They had associated with Jesus. They had seen His miracles, but they did not understand spiritual things until they had received the Holy Spirit.

They were not praying for the outpouring of the Holy Spirit, for they did not know what that meant.

They were not praying for power. How often we have read that into this scripture.

I remember reading Arthur's "Tongues of Fire." It is a marvelous book! Arthur describes this scene with the prayers of the one hundred and twenty awaiting for the power of God to fall upon them. He was playing with his imagination.

I want you to know two or three things that are vital.

Jesus did not tell the disciples anything, so far as we know, about what was going to happen in the Upper Room.

Neither did He tell them how to prepare themselves for it.

The Holy Spirit could not come any sooner than He did.

He came exactly when God planned it.

Their praying could neither bring the Holy Spirit, nor hinder Him from coming.

God did not ask them to repent of their sins, or have any special faith.

He required nothing only that they wait in the Upper Room until the promise of the Father came.

This is the climax of the Dream.

Redemption is at last consummated.

The Legal Side of that great Redemptive Charter has come into being.

Jesus, fresh from the terrible agony and torture of His Substitution, is entering the new Holy of Holies with His blood.

He has been absent on this mission for thirty odd years.

He is coming Home!

Such a Home-coming it is!

He is bearing His own blood.

He is now the High Priest of the New Covenant.

He is Man; He was a spirit before.

He will never lay aside His humanity.

Throughout Eternity He will be the God Man, the Head of the Church.

He is the first born of the New Creation People.

He is carrying His blood into the New Holy of Holies.

The Holy of Holies of the First Covenant has ceased to exist.

His blood is the red seal upon the Document of a perfect Redemption.

He has now made provision for the Recreating of the human race.

God is vindicated.

Man has accused God of creating him in the face of the fact that He must have known that he would fall.

Now He has paid the penalty of man's Transgressions, and man can receive Eternal Life and become the Righteousness of God in Christ.

What a battle it has been; but Love won.

≡||≡||≡||≡||≡||≡||≡||≡||≡||≡||≡||≡||≡||≡||≡||≡||≡||≡||≡

Chapter XII.

WHAT HAPPENED WHEN HE ENTERED WITH HIS BLOOD

HE spirit is hushed in the presence of that momentous event. There had never before been a moment like it. The Father had seen the Son nailed to the cross, but when sin touched Him, He turned His back upon Him.

The Son had not been in the Father's presence, so far as we know since that dread moment on the cross.

The Father had seen His suffering, had cried, "It is enough!" when the penalty was paid.

He had seen the Son recreated, brought back into fellowship with Himself, and witnessed that terrible combat with the dark forces of hell in which the Son stripped them of their authority, put off from Himself the principalities and powers and made a show of them, openly, triumphing over them.

But now the Son had come to the consummation of the entire drama.

He died as a Lamb. He suffered as a Substitute.

He had been made righteous in that dark region and conquered the adversary.

And as the Hero Lord, He arose from the dead.

But now He is the High Priest.

Carrying His blood into the Holy of Holies was the first work He ever did in the high priestly office.

He will not have to carry it in every year. It was a once for all sacrifice.

Satan had been conquered.

The claims of justice had been met.

Humanity had been redeemed.

God can now, on legal grounds, give eternal life to man.

Jesus had become the Saviour, He had dealt with man's Sin problem, and had settled it and saved man.

Man at last was ransomed. The debt was paid.

When Jesus sat down He entered into His rest, and automatically become the Minister of that New Sanctuary not made with human hands.

He had become the Mediator of the New Covenant.

What a wonderful thing that a New Covenant, sealed with the blood of God's own Son, would begin to function that day.

The first ministry was for the Son to carry His own blood, as the High Priest of the New Covenant, into the Holy of Holies.

As soon as that was done, and He was recognized as man's only Saviour, He became the saved man's Intercessor.

As Mediator, He stands between lost men and God. But as Intercessor He ever lives to make intercession for saved men.

He prays for them. He cares for them.

He had died for them.

He had made Redemption a possibility for them.

He had made it possible for them to receive Eternal Life.

Now He ever lives to minister to this New Creation and care for it.

He is not only the High Priest, Mediator, Saviour, Intercessor, but He is also their Heavenly Attorney, the Lord Advocate General.

"And if any man sin, we have an advocate with the Father, Jesus Christ, the righteous."

What a significant title!

When the believer sins, he loses the sense of Righteousness.

He loses the right of approach to the Father, but he has an advocate, and He is a righteous Advocate.

And when this believer has been caught in the toils of the adversary, and he cries for help and forgiveness, then Jesus takes his case, becoming his Advocate, and the fellowship is restored.

I John 1:9, "If we confess our sins, he is faithful and righteous to forgive us our sins, and to cleanse us from all unrighteousness."

I John 2:1-2, "My little children, these things write I unto you that ye may not sin. And if any man sin, we have an Advocate with the Father, Jesus Christ the righteous."

This is the most wonderful of all the ministries of the Man at God's right hand, but this is not all.

Hebrews 7:22 says, "He is the surety of the New Covenant." He is the guarantor of the entire New Testament from Matthew 1 to Revelation 22.

You see, behind this New Covenant is the integrity of the Father, and of Jesus and the Holy Spirit.

Their throne is back of every word.

You remember what He said to Abraham when that Old Covenant began to function, and He become the surety of the Old Covenant? "By myself have I sworn."

Now Jesus becomes the surety of the New Covenant.

Not only is He that, but He is our Lord High Priest.

He is the Bread Provider.

He is like a husband to a wife. Truly He is our Bride-groom and as the Lord Bride-groom, He provides our needs.

He watches over us, shields us from the enemy, is our protector.

The twenty-third Psalm is a perfect picture of the earth walk of the believer.

"The Lord is my shepherd," my bread-provider. How can I want? He causes me to "lie down in green pastures." I live in divine affluence. He knows every need of my life, and so I lie down, under His protection, in green pastures of plenty.

Sweet water flows by me, clear and sparkling as a crystal. I am the Jesus-cared-for one.

"He restoreth my soul." That means if there is anything that has frightened me, caused me to worry, filled me with fear, He restores my soul. He pulls me out of my fear and dread into rest and quietness.

And "He leadeth me in the paths" of this new kind of righteousness where I do not fear my enemies

The "paths of righteousness" are the paths of the New Creation.

And though I walk in the realm of spiritual death where everyone is ruled by the Adversary, "I shall fear no evil."

For I hear when He whispers "Lo, I am with you alway, even unto the end of the age."

"Thy rod" of protection and "thy staff" of plenty; "they comfort me." I am shielded, I am cared for, I am hidden away in Him. He is my protection .

But hear this. "Thou preparest a table before me in the presence of my enemies.

No-one can eat in the presence of enemies, for appetite is gone. But these are conquered enemies. These are bound enemies.

Where I have been defeated, conquered, and overcome, perhaps disgraced, I reign as a king in the realm of life through Jesus Christ my Lord.

"Thou anointest my head with oil." I have discovered that I am in the priesthood. I belong to the Royal family. For only they are anointed.

"My cup runneth over." I have joys unspeakable. This is a wonderful life I am living with my Lord.

And now, "goodness and mercy," the twins of grace, walk arm in arm with me along life's wonderful pathway.

I am dwelling in the presence of my Lord forever. Hallelujah!

This is just a little picture of the New Creation realities.

We have found the thing that the human heart has craved through all the ages.

When Jesus sat down, His work was finished, and He made me to sit down with Him.

You see, He raised me up with Him. He seated me with Him. I am one with Him.

He is the Head. I am part of the Body.

He is the Vine. I am a branch.

My life is hidden with Christ in God, my Saviour, my Lord.

My gracious, wonderful Saviour, High Priest, will come back by and by to receive me unto Himself.

The Father's heart is filled with joy, for in that Upper Room the Holy Spirit has given birth to the beginning of a new and mighty family.

Men who have been ruled by Satan are suddenly born again.

The angels look on this strange scene for they can see the heart life of man.

They witness the new birth of Peter, John, the mother of Jesus and all of the others.

Jesus was born in the manger thirty years before; and now the Holy Spirit has given birth in that Upper Room to one hundred and twenty men and women.

Demons look on with consternation.

They see a strange sight; the birth of one hundred and twenty Jesus men and women.

They have the nature of God. Within them now is the ability of God.

Every one of them becomes a master of the adversary and he knows it.

The Satan ruled man has become a son of God.

He has God's life and God's nature; now God can dwell in that man.

The body of every man who is born again becomes a tabernacle for the Holy Spirit.

The collective body of believers will be called the Temple of God.

A strange new thing has come to pass. The sin problem is settled for them, they have become New Creations, created in Christ Jesus.

They are the fruits of the three days and three nights of Christ's travail and spiritual agonies.

≡ǁǀǁ≡ǁǀǁ≡ǁǀǁ≡ǁǀǁ≡ǁǀǁ≡ǁǀǁ≡ǁǀǁ≡ǁǀǁ≡ǁǀǁ≡ǁǀǁ≡ǁǀǁ≡ǁǀǁ≡ǁǀǁ≡ǁǀǁ≡ǁǀǁ≡ǁǀǁ≡ǁǀǁ≡ǁǀǁ

Chapter XIII.

WHAT HAPPENED IN THE UPPER ROOM

ET US travel back to the Day of Pentecost where in the Upper Room one hundred and twenty men and women were born into the Family of God.

Everything had been prepared with Divine precision.

The Substitutionary Work of Christ was completed.

The Old Testament Saints had been taken from Paradise to Heaven.

The blood of the Lamb of God had been accepted.

Jesus sat down at the Right Hand of the Majesty on High.

The Holy Spirit left Heaven and came to earth to recreate men and women.

What a Day that must have been!

In regard to the birth of the Body of Christ certain facts should be noticed.

First, no faith was demanded.

They were not told they must repent.

They were not aware of what was going to take place.

No one had ever been Born Again.

They did not know that the First Covenant had been fulfilled and laid aside, and that a New Covenant was to take its place.

The fact that Circumcision had been displayed by the New Birth, was unknown to them.

No one knew that the Priesthood had stopped functioning.

They were ignorant of the fact that the Sacrifices, Atonements and Offerings, would no longer be accepted by Jehovah.

There was no longer an earthly Holy of Holies.

The Law of Moses was obsolete.

A New Covenant, a New Priesthood, and a New Law, had come into being.

"The old was nigh unto vanishing away."

The veil of the Temple had been rent from top to bottom.

Jehovah had left the earthly Holy of Holies for a New Temple; a Holy of Holies in Heaven.

They did not know that they had inherited a New Covenant, and were to be initiated into it by being recreated, born from above.

They had not awakened to the fact that it was to be a spiritual circumcision instead of physical.

The rent veil was not appreciated.

They could not comprehend its significance.

What took place on the Cross and during the three days and three nights was a closed book to them, nor had they any inkling as to what happened during the forty days.

They did not know that He had carried His blood into the Heavenly Holy of Holies.

They did not know that He was now their High Priest.

They had no intimation that the Lord whom they loved, was now seated at the right hand of the Majesty on High.

No one yet appreciated that God had a family, instead of a nation.

They did not appreciate the fact that they had a love Father instead of Jehovah.

The fellowship of bitter herbs was replaced with the sweet fellowship to be enjoyed with the Father, through Jesus Christ.

It is difficult for us to look back on that small company of men and women in the Upper Room, and think of them as Israelites with no conception of that which was to take place.

We must realize that everything that happened in the Upper Room aside from the Recreation was in the sense realm.

God had to work in both realms.

This was utterly new, everything connected with the First Covenant had been in the sense realm.

When the Spirit came they heard a rushing as of a mighty wind.

They saw the Tongues of Fire.

They heard each other speak in other tongues.

They did not know what had happened.

They were not aware of the fact that they had suddenly been born into the Family of God.

No one knew that they were New Creations.

They knew nothing of righteousness.

They knew nothing of Redemption.

They had arrived, but they did not know it.

They had received Eternal Life, they had the Holy Spirit dwelling in them, but none of them knew what it was all about.

They were filled with joy unspeakable and full of glory.

Heavenly peace filled their hearts.

They had Eternal Life.

They were the Righteousness of God.

They had a new Joy that no other human beings had ever possessed.

Every one of them could enter the Holy of Holies.

Not one of them was under condemnation.

They had the same Holy Spirit that had raised Christ Jesus from the dead.

They were ignorant of all these wonders, but they enjoyed them.

Let us look at it critically for just a moment.

According to Jesus and John the Baptist, they were to be immersed into the Holy Spirit.

I Cor. 12:13 explains what happened, "For in one Spirit were we all baptized into one body, whether Jew or Greek whether bond or free, and were all made to drink of one Spirit."

This explains what happened.

The moment they were immersed in the Spirit they were born of the Spirit.

You cannot be born unless you come out of a womb.

They came out of the womb of the Spirit.

He gave them birth in that Upper Room and they received Eternal Life.

Today when men and women receive Eternal Life, the Holy Spirit overshadows them as He did in that Upper Room, and imparts to their spirits, Eternal Life, the Nature of God.

It was the first time in human history, that a man received the Nature of God.

It is true that Jesus received Eternal Life before His resurrection but He is not classed with the others.

He was the "First Born from the Dead."

This is brought out in Col. 1:18, "And He is the Head of the body, the church, who is the beginning, the first born from the dead that in all things he might have the preeminence." Rom. 8:29.

A strange phenomenon took place.

Tongues of lambent fire rested on the head of each one of them.

This signified that the message that they were going to bring to the world would be given with relentless force.

Stephen proved this.

They could only deal with him by stoning him to death.

God gave these New Creation men a love Nature, His Nature, that could stand in the face of death and hatred, a victor.

This is a message that cannot be extinguished by the adversary. Why?

Because natural man is God hungry.

He is eternal life hungry.

He may not know it; he may not understand himself, but when he hears this message it stirs him to the very depths of his being.

The New Creation message is an answer to the heart-cry of the universal man.

Four mighty events took place in that Upper Room.

First, they were recreated.

Second, Tongues of Fire rested upon each one of them.

Third, the Holy Spirit entered their bodies.

Fourth, they spoke with other tongues.

They were the first to receive the Holy Spirit like this.

Under the First Covenant, the Holy Spirit would come upon men for a special ministry, but He always left them again.

They could not receive the Holy Spirit, as the disciples had in the Upper Room, for they were not born again.

The disciples were born again, thus the Holy Spirit could enter their bodies and make His permanent home there.

We have not realized it, but in the Upper Room the thing that Jesus prophesied had taken place.

God had left the Holy of Holies in the Temple.

The rent veil is a testimony of that fact.

The Spirit entered a new temple in that Upper Room, a Temple not made with hands.

I Cor. 3:16, "Know ye not that ye are the Temple of God, that the Spirit of God dwelleth in you? If any man destroys the Temple of God, him shall God destroy. For the temple of God is Holy, and such are ye." (or) which temple ye are. (Margin.)

Isn't it remarkable how the collective body is called the Temple, and that we are individually called tabernacles?

The moment the Holy Spirit entered their bodies and took them over, they began speaking in tongues.

What a thrilling moment that must have been !

Whether or not they all spoke in tongues, we do not know, but we do know that they all had received the Holy Spirit.

The multitudes that were gathered there were from many nations, yet each understood the message in his own tongue.

Whether the Holy Spirit interpreted the message to each individual, or gave to some members of that one hundred and twenty a special gift to speak other languages, we do not know.

We do know that the disciples were born again and indwelt of God.

The Love dream of the Father had come into being.

The legal side of the plan of redemption had been finished.

Now the vital side is seen.

The Father saw men and women receive eternal life and become sons and daughters.

The work of Jesus as a substitute was a success.

He saw the Holy Spirit give spiritual birth to men and women.

He saw them pass out of death into life, out of defeat into victory.

Common men had become overcomers.

He saw the reign of righteousness where condemnation had held full sway.

It was the beginning of the New Creation, a new era, a new class of men, God's own New Species.

It was the end of Sense Knowledge Rule.

The Abrahamic Covenant and everything that pertained to it was finished.

It was the beginning of a New Covenant in the Spirit.

This New Covenant was to unite the spirit of men with the Spirit of God.

A New Family had come into being, which consisted of sons and daughters who were indwelt, and taught of God.

It was a demonstration of what Eternal Life could do in a human being.

It was the outpouring of a New Kind of Love into the hearts of men.

The drama of the Upper Room was the Father's beginning of the greatest reality that ever came to human consciousness.

Men received Eternal Life.

Men were indwelt by God Himself.

Satan had been the master of the human race from the Fall to the cross.

On that cross he thought he had conquered the Man who had said, "Get thee behind me Satan."

That same Man had ordered the demons to "Come out of her."

On the cross, Satan believed he had that Man at his mercy.

For three days and three nights he caused that Man to suffer beyond anything that the human imagination can dream.

Then he saw that same Man free Himself from the Forces of Darkness, strip him of his dominion, paralyze the pangs of death and arise from the dead.

Now a strange phenomenon took place in the Upper Room.

He saw the Recreation of men and women.

He saw Sin stop being in their lives.

He saw the sins that they committed wiped out as though they had never been.

He saw the very nature of God come into their spirits and re-create them.

The image that Adam lost is seen in these recreated people.

They are Jesus men and women.

The Upper Room spells the Eternal defeat of Satan.

Satan must have been shocked.

He must have known that from that time on he would have a battle with men and women who had the authority that Jesus had unveiled.

Fear must have gripped his heart.

Chapter XIV

WHAT SATAN SAW ON THE DAY OF PENTECOST

ATAN had conquered Jesus on the Cross.

He had stirred the selfish hearts of the High Priesthood until in a jealous frenzy they had crucified Him.

The Father had laid on Him the sins of the world.

Jesus was left alone.

God turned His back on Him.

Satan triumphantly bore His Spirit to the Dark Regions of Hades.

All the sufferings and torments that Hell could produce were heaped upon Jesus.

When He had suffered Hell's agonies for three days and three nights, the Supreme Court of the Universe cried, "Enough."

He had paid the penalty and met the claims of Justice.

Satan saw Him Justified.

God made Him alive in Spirit right there in the presence of the cohorts of Hades.

Jesus was made a New Creation.

Rom. 8:29, "For whom he foreknew he also foreordained to be conformed to the image of his Son, that he might be the first born among many brethren."

Col. 1:18, "For he is the head of the body, the church; who is the beginning, the first born from the dead; that in all things he might have the preeminence."

Jesus was born into the New Covenant in Hades.

Col. 2:15 describes it in part, "Having put off from himself the principalities and the powers, he made a show of them openly, triumphing over them in it." (Marg.)

Satan was defeated.

Heb. 2:15, "And might deliver all them who through fear of death were all their lifetime subject to bondage."

Jesus paralyzed the death dealing authority of Satan.

He took captivity captive.

He defeated the Hosts of Hell, as our substitute.

In the Upper Room Satan witnessed the results.

He saw men and women recreated.

He saw them receive Eternal Life.

He saw their sins remitted, blotted out as though they had never been.

He saw the power and energy of the Holy Spirit in men.

He became aware of the fact that the New Creation people are his Masters.

He realized that these men and women had the authority to use the Name of Jesus.

These men and women in the Upper Room would be able to perform the same kind of miracles that Jesus had in His earth walk.

He must have remembered when Jesus said, "All authority has been given unto me in Heaven and on earth."

Jesus was the Master of Hell, and these New Creation people had received this authority.

He saw joy filled hearts, where tears had been their only drink.

He saw the defeated become Masters.

He saw his slaves shaking off their manacles.

He saw homes that had been filled with misery turned into miniature Heavens.

He saw his prisoners set free.

He saw men and women become New Creations.

These New Creations became Jesus men and women.

They counted the things that were not as though they were, and they leaped into being.

And they counted the things that were, as though they were not, and they ceased being.

He saw faith grow, where doubt and fear had held the throne for years.

He saw a New Race of men, a New Species come into being.

He saw the New Birth take place.

He saw God take men out of his grip and fill their hearts with love, where hatred had reigned supreme.

He saw selfishness curtailed.

He saw Righteousness become a reality.

The strangest phenomenon was to see men and women stand in the presence of God without the sense of guilt, inferiority, or condemnation.

This shook the very foundation of Hell.

A new language was spoken in the New Creation Family.

A language permeated with love words.

He saw men reign as Kings in this New Realm of Life.

He saw this New Kind of Love gain mastery over men.

Satan slew Jesus to annihilate Him, instead of that, His death and resurrection gave birth to this New Creation Family.

They multiplied so rapidly that he realized he must destroy them before they destroyed him.

I was asked, "Do you think Satan knew about all this before?"

"Didn't he know what Christ was doing on the Cross?"

"Didn't he know that if Christ went to Hell He would conquer him?"

Eph. 3:9-10 Am. Rev. "And to make all men see what is the dispensation of the mystery which for ages has been hid in God who created all things; to the intent that now unto the principalities and the powers in the heavenly places might be made known through

90

the church the manifold wisdom of God, according to the eternal purpose which he purposed in Christ Jesus our Lord."

Now notice this wonderful fact, the mighty plan of Redemption was sealed between the Father and Jesus to be revealed at an appointed time.

Satan knew nothing of it.

Satan now sees that he is defeated.

Every time he destroyed a Christian it gave birth to another.

He feared God's Word on the lips of these New Creation men more than anything he had ever faced.

He must destroy the Word.

Where ever they were permitted to preach in that Name it gave birth to Jesus men and women.

During the seven hundred years known as the Dark Ages, Satan had smothered the Word.

Luther gave birth to it again.

In many Countries today, the Word has apparently been stamped out; however it still remains in the hearts of some men and women.

Satan saw that these Jesus men and women fed on the Word, and in doing so they became more and more like the Master.

To destroy the Word then, would stop their increase.

Now he knows his work.

You can now see what our ministry is, we must give this living Word to men and women, nothing else can take its place.

If Heaven ever had a Holiday it was when the miracle took place in the Upper Room.

It was when the Father, Jesus and the Holy Spirit saw the first born child of the great Substitutionary Sacrifice of Christ.

The angels must have looked on in perfect wonderment.

You and I can only see the external, but they could see the internal man Recreated in Christ Jesus.

They could see the thing that the Father had dreamed of throughout the ages, come to pass.

We do not know how He loved us.

He so loved us, when we were ruled by the Devil, that He sacrificed His Son to make it possible for us to receive Eternal Life.

If the Church should ever catch a glimpse of how dear and beautiful they are to the Father, it would transform them.

The angels themselves became their custodians. They walked with them, they cared for them, they protected them and shielded them from danger.

I have wondered how Jesus looked upon the New Creations, and how He felt toward them.

He had loved them in His earth walk, now they are New Creations; they are Redeemed with His own blood.

How priceless they must be to Him.

You remember how Paul put it, "He loved me and gave Himself up for me." I believe that if we knew how much the Master loved us, we would make that same confession.

≡II≡II≡II≡II≡II≡II≡II≡II≡II≡II≡II≡II≡II≡II≡II≡II≡II≡II≡III

Chapter XV

WHAT THE NEW CREATION MEANT IN HEAVEN

F YOU could visualize what took place on the Day of Pentecost in the three Worlds, it would unveil to your heart one of the greatest miracles in Human history.

I wonder what effect it had upon the Father and Jesus?

Christ had gone through Hell to make this day possible.

The Father had suffered a thousand Hells seeing the suffering of His Son, to make this day possible.

You ask, "what happened?"

Why, the Family of God was instituted; it came into being.

The first born Children of the New Race of men came into being in that Upper Room.

God had lost His Man in the Garden, now He found Him again in the Upper Room.

The New Creation had come into being.

Sons and Daughters of God had been born.

God was a Father at last.

Jesus was a real Saviour.

He had never been a Saviour before.

He had been the Creator, God manifested in the flesh.

He had been the great fulfiller of the Old Covenant and all that pertained to it.

He had been the substitute.

For three days and three nights He had gone through the agonies of the Eternities to redeem man and justify God.

He had satisfied the claims of Justice; thus the Father God had the right on that wonderful Day to give man His own Nature.

Those one hundred men and women were born into the family of God.

Jesus not only became a Saviour, but He is our seated Lord at the right hand of the Father, a Mediator between God and Man.

Not only that, but when man was Born Again into the Family of God, He became his Intercessor, ever living to pray for him.

What a ministry the Incarnation started, the heart can hardly grasp it.

He is not only the Great Intercessor, the head of the Prayer League of the ages, and example for all praying men, but He is their Advocate.

When trouble comes and we yield for a moment to the Adversary, we have an Advocate, at the right hand of the Majesty on High.

He is our Attorney General.

He is the Great Master, Christ my Lord.

But that is not all.

On that wonderful Day of Pentecost, He became the head of the Body, that new Temple that was to be erected of living stones: that strange new thing, that New Species of men; that new type of Jesus men.

He is the Head.

He is the Lord of the Church.

He is the Caretaker, the Bread-provider, the Shield and Protector.

How that term Caretaker, thrilled my heart.

He cares for me.

He watches over me.

He knows my every need and desire.

My own Lord.

But the picture would not be complete if I did not call your attention to this fact, that He is the surety, the guarantor of the New Covenant.

His Throne is back of this Covenant.

That Throne is the security of the New Covenant in His blood.

What a seal there is upon that Throne, the blood of the Son of God.

Now we are able to speak of God as our Father.

He has always been a Father.

Through all eternity, there has been a Father heart longing for children.

It took Him ages to create this world of ours as a home for His man.

The earth was the love nest of the heart of God for His family.

It took Him ages to store it with minerals, metals, gasses and oil for His man to enjoy.

What a Father hearted God He is.

We catch glimpses of that great heart in the four gospels, but a full flowering of it is seen in the Epistles.

Words cannot describe it, for we live in a sense knowledge world surrounded by sense knowledge images.

All of our reactions have been through sense knowledge conceptions.

What a Heavenly Day that must have been when the family of God came into being.

What anthems the angels must have sung!

What choruses must have re-echoed through the celestial spaces on that glorious new creation birthday; the day the New Covenant began to operate on earth, if we may express it that way.

You see the Covenant was between Jesus and the Father.

The Church is the Beneficiary of that wonderful Document.

It proved that the Blood of Christ had been accepted and that the Sacrifice was sufficient.

The New Covenant Law came into being.

These men received the Nature of God.

Love became a natural thing.

Love actually leaped into being.

It is no wonder that men no longer claimed their own, but had all things in common.

The old order of things died out when the Veil of the Temple was rent, and God abandoned the earthly Holy of Holies, and entered into the Heavenly Holy of Holies.

The Holy Spirit had recreated one hundred and twenty men and women.

In that Upper Room, the Church, the Body of Christ was formed.

That Body is the Temple of the Holy Spirit.

Jerusalem had its Temple where the great sacrifices were made. Then too, it had its little Tabernacles where the people gathered for inspiration and fellowship.

Our bodies are the little tabernacles where the Spirit gives us inspiration and fellowship through the Word.

The Angels had a new ministry.

They had ministered to the servants of Jehovah, now they were to minister to the Sons and Daughters of God.

Their previous state as mediator between Jehovah and man was now lost.

Jesus is now the Great Mediator.

Every Son and Daughter of God has a legal right to enter the Holy of Holies.

At the time of that First Covenant, only the High Priest could enter, and he but once a year.

Now we, as Sons and Daughters, can enter as we will.

We may enter to worship.

We may enter to make our petitions.

We may enter for fellowship.

And we may enter, simply to come together in love.

The Holy Spirit's ministry was first to Recreate.

He gives birth to Sons and Daughters of God.

He brings conviction to their hearts.

He shows them what Eternal Life can do for them.

He reveals to them how much better the Heavenly Father would be to them, than Jehovah of the Old Covenant.

He was not only going to show the vast difference between their life and the life in Christ, but He was to reveal to them the great possibilities that would come to man after he had received Eternal Life.

The great effect it would have upon their children, was revealed by Him.

He unveiled to this New Man what it would mean to walk in

love, to live as the Master lived.

He let these men know that they had become partakers of the Divine Nature.

Perhaps the greatest reward these New Creation men could receive, was the realization that they could bring joy to the Great Father Heart of God.

The Father could feel the same thrill over His Children as earthly parents feel towards their offspring.

What a ministry He had to bring us into a conscious knowledge of our relationship and of our privileges and rights in the family of God.

He now has God's program to carry out in the world and He is to work through a new race of men.

If God told Adam to conquer and subdue the earth, not replenish it as the old version reads, what a ministry this new creation man has in subduing selfishness, viciousness and bitterness with love, peace and joy.

A new kind of man and a new kind of love.

I can remember what Jesus said in John 13:34-35, "A new commandment I give unto you that ye love one another, even as I have loved you, that ye also love one another. By this shall all men know that ye are my disciples, if ye have love one for another."

A love race.

A love Covenant.

A love commander.

A love family.

The day of hardness and selfishness ends in love.

These last twenty-five years of dreadful wars, have so blinded our consciousness of right and wrong, and love and joy, that we can hardly take this truth in, but the dream of the Father was that love should dominate and rule every one of us.

You see there are two major forces in the world; selfishness, and love.

Selfishness has given birth to all our sorrows, heartaches and tears. It has caused all the wars and other atrocities in which men take part.

The world is not yet acquainted with the new kind of love, Agapa love.

Few have seen it in practice, and still fewer enjoy its fulness.

It absolutely eliminates selfishness.

For years I wondered what Spiritual Death was.

I knew that Spiritual Life was the Nature of the Father.

I knew that Spiritual Death must be the Nature of Satan.

Then I saw that the Nature of the Father is revealed through our conduct, our acts of love.

Like a flash I saw it, Satan's Nature is selfishness.

96

God so loved that He gave.

Satan was so selfish that he sought to rob God and the human race of everything worth while.

Selfishness is a robber.

It had reigned without a rival through the ages.

Now a mighty new Force has broken into the Sense Realm.

That mighty Force is Love. (Read my book "The New Kind of Love.")

It heads up in God.

It was unveiled in Christ.

It is becoming operative in us.

Love without the ability to use it would not be so good.

That is why Jesus has been made unto us Wisdom.

Wisdom is the ability to use the knowledge of all these things of which we have been speaking.

Wisdom is God's efficiency and ability, given to man.

Wisdom is the ability to use knowledge to advantage.

Wisdom is seen in every detail of creation.

All the wonderful gasses, minerals, and oils that are concealed in the earth and sea, would never have been discovered, had God not given to the New Creation the Wisdom to find them.

What we have to recognize is, that it is man's Spirit that is re-created

This Spirit is the real man.

This Spirit gives birth to all creative ability.

Whether it be in the inventive, literary, artistic, or musical line, the ability comes from the same source.

You might say they are born of one womb, the Recreated Spirit.

That is not all that is born from this marvelous mother of science and art, but love and joy are also her offspring.

She is called the heart of the human spirit.

The Natural human spirit cannot give birth to these things.

That is the reason that the Nations who have never received Eternal Life are backward, without creative ability.

They do not have the New Kind of Love, which is born from the New Kind of Life, that Jesus brought to the World.

We are standing now on the other side of His great Substitutionary Work for the New Creation.

We are looking at the men and women who have been born from Above.

These people have received the life and nature of God.

What is available to them now?

Are there some hidden secrets and truths that have been kept from us?

What effect would they have on our lives if we were conscious of them?

Everything the Father did in Christ belongs to us.

"He has blessed us with every spiritual blessing in the Heavenlies in Christ."

We have a right to the wisdom that Jesus used in His earth walk.

He has been made unto us Wisdom, to teach us to use the ability that has been given to us.

"Of His fulness have we all received."

Now we have the ability to use that fulness to enter into all the riches of His finished work.

But one of the rarest blessings that has come to us, is that we can make the heart of the Father glad in our daily walk.

We can bless Him.

Chapter XVI

WHAT WAS AVAILABLE TO MAN

HEN Jesus sat down at the Right Hand of the Father, the Sin Problem was settled.

The Sinner Problem had yet to be individually settled. The great Problem of man's Redemption was completed.

Jesus had satisfied the claims of Justice.

He had conquered Satan, and stripped him of his authority.

He made it possible for men, who were under bondage to Satan, to become independent of the Adversary.

The bitter accusations hurled at God, for creating man in the face of the fact that He knew he would fall, could no longer continue.

God answered the cry of Universal Man, by making His own Son the Substitute, paying the penalty of all of man's transgressions.

In other words, a New Kind of fellowship.

Fellowship with God Himself.

When this was done, God had a legal right to give man His own Nature.

That was the only solution for the Sin Problem.

If God could, on legal grounds, give Eternal Life to man, then man could come out of the thralldom of Satan and become a Master man.

God had a legal right to make man a New Creation.

Forgiving man's sin and then leaving him would be of no avail, for man would go right on sinning.

God must make man a New Creation.

He must eliminate the thing from his nature that had made him a subject of Satan, and impart to him His own nature which will make him righteous.

All of this must be based on legal grounds.

Man is legally a child of the Adversary; he must legally become a child of God.

In some way God must make this man Righteous.

Man must be able to stand in the presence of God without the sense of guilt, inferiority, or condemnation.

At the same time all fear must be taken out, enabling him to stand in the presence of Satan without the sense of inferiority.

This can only be done by the impartation of God's Nature to him.

There must be a Recreation of his spirit.

He cannot have two Natures, for that would hold him in bondage.

He must be made a complete, perfect, New Man.

He must be a New Creation.

II Cor. 5:17 tells us, "Wherefore if any man is in Christ, there is a new creation, the old things have passed away; behold they have become new, and all these things are of God, who has reconciled us unto himself, through the death of his Son."

God made provisions, through the Substitutionary Sacrifice of His own Son, to make a New Man over whom Satan would have no dominion.

In fact this New man becomes the Master over the Dark Forces of the Black Prince.

Perhaps the most wonderful fact of all is that God made it possible for the Holy Spirit to come into a recreated man's body and make His home there.

It is a marvelous thing for God to be with man, assisting him in all of his hard places, but Jesus said, "He (the Holy Spirit) is with you and shall be in you." Jn. 14:17.

Not only was God to dwell in man, but there is another wonderful truth.

Jesus the Substitute, came to make it possible for men to live together, and be loyal to each other, without fear.

Fellowship with one another.

Fellowship with His living Word.

You understand, fellowship means sharing equally.

In this New Brotherhood there are no dictators.

We all serve one another.

The slave and the master are on equal terms.

That was the dream of the Father for His Family.

It is the end of Sense Rule.

The Recreated human spirit is to dominate the New Creation man.

All the world's great leaders have been Sense Knowledge men.

Now we are to be Spiritual leaders.

Christ is the Head of the Church, and the Head of the Body.

He is to rule the New Creation man through the spirit.

Wisdom

One of the most distinctive features about this New man, is his Wisdom.

He possesses a New Kind of Wisdom.

The earthly wisdom is sensual, selfish, and Devilish. Jas. 3:15.

It is the wisdom of Satan, himself.

You see that in the present war.

The New Kind of Wisdom is gentle, easy to be entreated, dominated by love, permeated with gentleness, and joy.

We learn in this book that the Creative ability is in the recreated human Spirit.

God has taken over man in this New Creation.

He has imparted to us His own Nature.

His Creative ability has given us our marvelous Mechanical, Medical, and Chemical ages.

What an age it has been.

I must not neglect to call your attention to another Divine gift to the New man, that is, Peace.

The world knows nothing about this Peace.

It is a quiet rest.

A sense of being shut in with Him, with His protection and care.

Not only has this New man a Peace that passeth all understanding, but he has a Joy that is unspeakable and full of glory.

Happiness comes from our environment and surroundings, our physical pleasures.

Joy is an inward thing.

It belongs only to the Recreated Spirit.

It is the dominating element of the New Life.

It brings man into a rest.

You have a sense of utter safety, for your Father is watching over you.

He climaxes all this, by imparting to man a New Kind of Love; His own very Nature, which operates through this New Creation Man.

This chapter may surprise you.

Your Tenses become your dearest helps or your worst enemies.

If you are going to get your heart's desire in the future it will never materialize.

You say, "I am going to get my healing. I know that Christ bore my disease, and I have a right to it."

That does not affect your disease.

Your Tenses have taken you prisoner.

If you say, "I know that He bore my disease, and I thank Him for it, I know by His stripes I am healed," the Tenses are working with you now.

When you know clearly the difference between the Legal and the Vital aspects of Redemption, you will have solved one of your most difficult problems.

The Legal is what God has done for you in Christ.

The Vital is what the Holy Spirit does in you through the Word.

You will not find that confession by surrendering or consecrating or even fasting, it is only when you begin to act on the Word that it is yours.

Begin to act as though you already possess it, make your confession that you do possess it, that it is yours now.

If you will practice it, this chapter will give you your "Promised Land."

Chapter XVII

WHY THE TENSES WHIP US

E HAVE never realized that the tenses are often ruled by the senses.

Most of our popular hymns are in the future or in the past tense.

Our leaders tell us what we ought to be and what we ought to do.

They tell us what we should strive to get, but they seldom tell us how to get it.

I don't know whether you have ever thought of it or not, but everything in the spiritual realm that the believer needs to make him a success belongs to him.

We have sung, "I Surrender All" and "All is on the Altar," not realizing that when we took Christ as our Saviour, we confessed Him as our Lord.

Rom. 10:9-10 "Because if thou shalt confess with thy mouth Jesus as Lord, and shalt believe in thy heart that God raised Him from the dead, thou shalt be saved: for with the heart man believeth unto righteousness; and with the mouth confession is made unto salvation."

Notice this carefully that he confesses the Lordship of Jesus.

If he does that, he hasn't anything to surrender, as he comes to recognize the fact that he is not his own, he was bought with a price (I Cor. 6:20), and you can't very well surrender something that doesn't belong to you, nor lay something on God's altar that is not yours to give.

You belong to Him.

Not only do you belong to Him by your own consent; you are like a wife that consents in the wedding ceremony. She gives herself to that man. She doesn't have the wedding service repeated day after day. She belongs to him.

The believer belongs to Christ.

It is a once for all union.

That is in the past tense. The thing is done.

It was consummated when you received Eternal Life and became a New Creation in Christ Jesus.

When you recognize that, you grow to know the reality of it so that you live daily in the consciousness of your union with Him; of your oneness with Him.

He is yours; you are His.

All that He wrought for you in His substitutionary sacrifice, is yours.

You don't have to struggle to get it.

You don't have to surrender for it.

You don't have to pray for it.

It is yours as much as your hands are yours, as much as your feet are yours.

All our struggling, our praying and fasting to get power, is useless and it has built up within us a type of unbelief that is very difficult to overcome.

Eph. 3:20 "Now unto him that is able to do exceeding abundantly above all that we ask or think, according to the power that worketh in us."

The word "power" there, means "ability."

We will translate it like this: "According to the ability of God that is at work within us."

And Phil. 2:13 says, "It is God who is at work within us."

If you have God in you, you have the power house in you.

If you have Him in you, and you yield to His ability, let Him control you, everything that you need is there on tap ready for use.

I used to consecrate and surrender to the Lord daily.

I found out after a while I was running in a circle.

I was doing the same thing day after day.

I was not making any progress.

Many of our spiritual leaders have worked on a philosophy of failure.

It is based on unbelief.

They teach us to doubt, unconsciously.

They haven't recognized that there are two phases of redemption, the legal, and the vital.

The legal is always in the past.

It is what God did for us in the past in the Great Substitution.

He redeemed us.

Our redemption is in the past tense.

He doesn't have to redeem us again.

The moment that you confessed Christ and acknowledged His lordship you became a New Creation.

You see that moment the Father imparted His own nature to you, so you are now by nature a child of God.

That is in the past.

That cannot be done again.

We are now in Christ, one with Him, a branch of the Vine. That is past.

You ask the Holy Spirit to come in and occupy His New Creation.

All that God is doing in you in the New Creation is vital.

When you understand the difference between the legal and the vital side of redemption, you will be able to take advantage of what has been done for you; of what He is doing in you, through the Holy Spirit, by the Word; and what Jesus is now doing for you at the Right

Hand of the Father.

The failure of the believer can usually be laid to the lack of clear apprehension of what he actually is in Christ.

When he can quietly say, "I am a New Creation; I have in me now the life, the nature of my Father God; I am a partaker of His love nature; all I need then to enable me to walk in love is to let His nature dominate me."

Someone may ask: "Well how can I do that?"

That is easy. Just begin to practice or to act upon the Word.

You see, believing is acting upon what He has asked you to do.

There is no believing without acting.

Faith is a noun. You have acted.

You have arrived, and on the ground of that, you begin to take your place as a son, as a daughter in the family of God.

You have back of you His living Word, and back of the Word is His Throne, and back of the Throne is God Himself.

You are quite safe.

When you know this as you know addition and subtraction, you will have a fearless confession.

You will dare to tell the world what you are, and what you can do.

You will be able to say with perfect fearlessness: "When I pray the Father hears me."

You are not afraid to say: "Greater is He that is in me than any circumstance that may confront me, any difficulty that may confront me. I become the master of circumstances in Christ. I have come to recognize the reality of His indwelling and have become God-in-side-minded."

You understand what I mean? We became automobile minded. We no longer think of walking or hiring a team. We go out and get into the car and go to our destination.

Some of us have become air minded. Instead of writing, we telegraph or we call them up on the phone, or we get into a plane and go hurtling through the sky at two or three hundred miles an hour.

Now we become Word-minded.

The Word means exactly what it says.

When I read it, it is His present tense message to my heart, for the Word is always Now.

The Father is always Now.

Jesus is my Now Lord, and so I am building into myself by the aid of the Holy Spirit, the reality of the Word.

This is the vital side, you see, of what He is doing in me.

He builds Himself into me; He and the Word are one.

As He builds Himself into me, He builds His faith into me;

He builds His wisdom into me. Jesus is made unto me wisdom

from God. I Cor. 1:30.

As the heart absorbs these real things, the mind becomes renewed and comes into fellowship with the Recreated spirit.

That will mean that you are in fellowship with the Word, and with the Father.

There will be no limit to you now.

You are tied up with Him.

His ability has become your ability

Yes, He is yours.

All that He is, He is in you, and you begin to take advantage of it.

You have discovered that you have a disease in your body that makes you unable to work. You say, "I can't do this work because I haven't strength to do it."

You say, "I can't go there because I haven't the ability to go; I can't do this: I can't do that."

Thus you build up within yourself elements upon which your disease feeds, your sickness feeds, and your doubts and fears feed, until after a while they have gained absolute supremacy over you.

You are now helpless.

Your confession adds fuel on which they feed, and they are burning up your resistance.

You must recognize this fact. You are a New Creation.

You have God's life in you and you have the great Mighty Holy Spirit who raised Jesus from the dead within, and if the Spirit who raised Jesus from the dead dwells in you, He will bring the Father's life in fulness into you until it draws out the disease, or the doubts, or the fears.

It will bring you into the very strength of God.

You remember II Cor. 5:4, the last clause, "that what is mortal may be swallowed up of life."

That life is God's life; the Greek word is "Zoe."

God's life pours into your physical body and destroys the diseases in it.

If Jesus tarries, we will all die physically, but while we are living, He plans that these bodies be healthy and strong.

Sometimes when I have prayed for people where there have been operations and part of some member of the body has been taken away, they could feel the life of God come pouring into them and there came a recreation of that lost portion.

I prayed for a man whose spine had been crushed. The vertebrae had been destroyed so that there was no form to them; when we prayed for them, a new spine was created, a perfect spine, so that just in a few moments, he took his steel jacket off and could bend his body in any way.

Or take another case. A man had a rupture. He suffered with it for sixteen years. He wore a steel belt. He lived in continual pain while he worked. The instant he acted on the Word, that rupture closed up and his body became perfectly normal. He took the steel belt off and was perfectly well.

You see that is acting on the Word.

That is present tense consciousness.

No religion about it.

It is the living Word becoming a reality in our consciousness.

Now you understand what it means when we put these things in the future and we put hope in the place of faith.

I say, I hope I will get my healing.

I am sure that I will have it some time.

There is no value in that confession.

It is only a delusion.

It is not faith.

This is merely sense knowledge hope, but now I know the Word, and if I pray, I get it.

I know Jesus bore this disease.

I know that Isaiah 53:4-6 is an absolute fact. "Surely he hath borne our sicknesses and carried our pains, and we have come to esteem him as the one who was stricken, smitten of God, and afflicted (with our diseases). He was wounded for our transgressions, He was bruised for our iniquities; the chastisement of our peace was upon Him; and with his stripes we are healed.

Put this in the first person singular and it simplifies it.

Surely He hath borne my diseases and my pains, and I have come to appreciate this.

I know that it is done.

You see the moment that a man accepts Christ, he enters into all this.

Jesus bore his diseases just the same as He bore our sins.

He is not troubled with his old sins.

The moment that he accepted Christ, they were all remitted.

The same thing is true with his diseases.

Supposing that after one has been recreated and his old sins have all been remitted, wiped out as though they had never been, that he permits the adversary to camouflage the whole thing and bring back the memory of his old life and hold it over him continually.

He loses peace.

He loses the sense of fellowship with the Father.

He loses the consciousness of righteousness.

He goes into the blackest doubts and fears.

He should never allow the adversary to do that.

The adversary cannot put his old diseases back on him or in him.

The adversary cannot put his old nature back in him.

This was all done away when he was recreated.

In the same manner the adversary camouflages our diseases and holds us in bondage.

He can so camouflage them that they become a reality to us and we lose the consciousness of our healing, and Satan becomes our master.

Here is where we want to learn the secret of the power of words as well as actions.

Heb. 4:14, "Having then a great high priest, who hath passed through the heavens, Jesus the Son of God, let us hold fast our confession."

Your old version reads profession. Confession is much better.

Christianity is a confession. Why? Because it is a faith thing, and faith depends upon your confession.

You have seen that your healing was wrought in Christ, in His great Substitution.

The Father actually laid upon His spirit your diseases.

That cancer, that tumor, that T.B. was laid upon the Master's spirit, and He became sick with it and on the cross He was the sickest being the universe ever knew.

He not only had our sins put upon Him, being made sin with our sins, but He was made sick with our diseases.

So in the mind of the Father, I Pet. 2:24 is true, "Who His own self bare our sins in His own body on the tree, that we, being dead to sins, should live unto righteousness; by whose stripes ye were healed."

That is how the Father looks upon you.

Your sins and diseases have been put away.

You have become the righteousness of God in Christ.

You have become perfectly healed in His Substitutionary Work.

When you find this out, in the face of the fact that the cancer is still there, you begin to praise the Father for your perfect healing, your sense ruled friends cannot understand you. They think you are beside yourself.

You are not, but by faith you are now taking your stand and you are confessing what you really are in Christ, and in the face of pain you hold fast to your confession.

In the face of everything, you hold fast to that fact that He said you are healed, and, if He said you are healed, you are.

You dare say aloud, "I am what He says I am. I can do what He says I can do. He says I can come boldly to the Throne of Grace and have my prayers answered. He says that I have authority over all the power of the enemy, and that I am a master of demons and a master of sickness in the name of Jesus Christ, His Son, and I know He can't lie. I know that what He says is true. I boldly take my stand, and in the face of everything that may come, I hold fast to my confession."

Now you live in the present tense.

He is what He says He is, and you are what He says you are.

His Word cannot lie, and you hold fast to that Word in your confession.

If you are afraid to make your confession, the adversary takes advantage of it.

If you waver in your confession, one moment you say it is true, and the next moment you listen to the senses, the adversary takes advantage of you.

But you say, "Would it not be untrue for me to say that I am healed, when I am not?"

No, you see there are two kinds of truth.

There is Revelation Truth, the Bible, especially the Pauline Epistles, with which we are dealing, and then, there is sense knowledge truth.

I find that Revelation Truth teaches me that my swollen ankle is healed.

I discover it as a man discovers gold, and I am filled with exaltation and joy, and I joyfully say to my friends: "See this, 'By His stripes I am healed'."

And my friends say: "That is foolish; why you see the ankle is still swollen."

"Yes, I know it, but the Word declares that He laid that disease on Jesus, and what God says, is true."

I hold fast to my confession, and the adversary loses his dominion over my body, and I become perfectly normal and well.

Now I know the difference between faith and hope.

Now I know that hope is a good waiter, but a poor receiver.

≡‖

Jesus illustrated in His daily walk the things that the Prophets attempted to express.

He was like His Father, He did things with words.

He taught us how to use words, how to fill them with authority and power.

The most outstanding thing to my heart in the life of the Master, was the authority that He exercised through words.

He gave us a new conception of the value of words.

He taught us another lesson, the value of Righteousness.

Jesus had no sense of lack or need.

I believe that it was the Father's desire that we should be like Jesus.

That we should use our Righteousness so that we can come into His presence without any Sin consciousness; and stand in the presence of Satan or his works without a sense of inferiority.

Jesus' confession is another staggering example of His faith in Himself.

"I am the bread of life."

"I am the light of life, he that followeth me shall not walk in the darkness but shall have the light of life."

He challenged us at every point.

Again He said, "I came out from the Father. I came into the world again I leave the world and go unto the Father."

He knew who He was.

He knew what He was.

He knew why He came.

≡‖

Chapter XVIII

THE JESUS OF THE FOUR GOSPELS

ERE is a statement that the Master made, Jn. 14:12, "He that believeth on me, the works that I do shall he do also; and greater works than these shall he do; because I go unto my Father."

This statement bothered me a great deal.

I wondered what He meant.

It seemed to me in those early days of my ministry, that He was intimating that we were to perform greater miracles than He had.

At that time Sense Knowledge teachings governed me largely.

However I was never satisfied with that interpretation.

One day the truth dawned on me.

We were to do another type of miracle.

These miracles were to take place in the Spirit Realm, and these were greater than those performed in the Physical Realm.

We were to lead men and women to Christ, and they would receive Eternal Life.

Our miracles would be connected with the recreation of men and women.

The miracles of Jesus were all performed in the Sense Realm.

The Disciples and followers of Jesus believed only in the things that they saw, heard, felt, or experienced in the physical realm.

Their knowledge was bound by the senses.

God sent His Son into the Sense Realm so that men could witness His miracles, and behold Him as a man.

"He was God manifested to the senses." I Tim. 3:16.

John 1:14, "And the Word became flesh, and dwelt among us and we beheld his glory as of the only begotten from the Father, full of grace and truth.

The Word came into the Realm of the Senses.

The disciples had followed Him during the three years of His public ministry.

They witnessed His miracles.

Jesus had controlled the winds and the waves.

He had actually walked upon the Sea of Galilee, as easily as we walk on pavement.

They had witnessed His compassion for the multitude.

He was in reality, Love manifested to the senses.

He possessed wisdom beyond natural man.

He knew men, as we would say, from the ground up.

They had heard His teaching.

They were thrilled by His words.

They had seen miracles take place day after day.

He healed people with words.

He raised the dead with words.

He made the bread to increase with words.

He turned water into wine with words.

They said of Him, "No man ever spake as He."

One of the greatest revelations He brought into the Sense Realm was the authority and power that could be invested in words.

They had witnessed a new way of living.

It was the Love Way, yet no one understood it.

It is not likely that anyone attempted to imitate it.

This was a new way of life.

When Jesus said "I am the way the truth and the life," no one understood what He meant.

He had another prerogative if we may call it that, it was His ability to enter into the Father's presence without the sense of guilt or unworthiness.

The multitudes that thronged about Him feared God.

They had been taught to fear Him.

They knew the dread experienced by the High Priest when he entered the Holy of Holies once a year, on the behalf of the sins of Israel.

They were astonished when Jesus called the God of the Jews, Father.

He seemed on intimate terms with their Jehovah.

At the tomb of Lazarus, they heard Him say, "Father I thank thee that thou hearest me always."

They could sense a Divine intimacy between Jesus and the Father, that staggered them.

We, as New Creations, can look back on the earth walk of the Master and notice certain limitations in His miraculous life.

It is hard to conceive of limitations in the walk of the limitless One.

He controlled the laws of nature as a general would control an army.

Every law as far as we know was subjected to His will.

In spite of the fact that He could heal the sick bodies of men, He could not heal their spirits.

He could forgive sins as they were forgiven under the law, but He could not remit sins as they were remitted after His death and Resurrection.

He could impart natural life (psuche) but He could not give to them Eternal Life, (Zoe).

He had said, "I am come that you may have life, and have it abundantly."

He told them "He that believeth on me shall pass out of death into life."

He meant that they were to pass out of the Realm of Spiritual Death into the Realm of Spiritual Life.

This could not occur as long as Jesus lived.

He could not recreate them.

He could not say, "If you believe on me I will give you Eternal Life."

He could not say, "I will recreate you, I will make you New Creations."

Some one asked, "Didn't the Disciples believe on Him?"

"Didn't Mary and Martha, believe on Him?"

Yes, in a way they believed on Him; but what did they believe?

Did they believe that "He had died for their sins according to the Scripture; that they had life through His Name?"

Did they believe that He was the Mediator between God and man?

No.

They believed that He was the Son of God, their Messiah.

They knew nothing of His Substitutionary Sacrifice.

They did not know that He was going to die on the Cross as their Sin Substitute.

They did not know that He was going to arise from the dead and carry His Blood into the Heavenly Holy of Holies.

They were ignorant of all these truths.

It is deeply important that the believer understands the difference between the faith that men had in Jesus in His earth walk, and the faith that we have in Him now as our Lord, Saviour, and Substitute.

Jesus could not make them Righteous.

Loving them as He loved them, still He did not have the authority to make them Righteous, which would enable them to stand in the presence of God without the sense of guilt, condemnation, or inferiority.

He could heal their diseases, but He could not change their Natures.

He could cast demons out of their bodies.

He could break the power of demons over their physical bodies.

He could not redeem them from the authority of Satan, and from condemnation and judgment.

He could not give them the ability to fellowship with the Father.

Despite His intense love for them they could not fellowship with Him.

They were spiritually dead.

They had not yet passed from death into life.

I Cor. 1:9, "God is faithful, through whom ye were called into the fellowship of his Son Jesus Christ our Lord."

They were called to be Disciples, Students, and Apostles, but not until His death and resurrection, were they called into fellowship with Him.

If you will recall in John 15:14-15 in the last address of the Master, He spoke these words, "Ye are my friends, if ye do the things which I command you. No longer do I call you servants; for the servant knoweth not what his lord doeth: but I have called you friends; for all things that I heard from my Father, I have made known unto you." He could call them friends but not brethren. It is important that you make this distinction in your mind. Jesus is not our friend today. He is our Lord and Saviour. A friend is someone outside of the family.

Most teachings have contended that the Disciples were Christians when they walked with Jesus before His death, just because He called them friends.

They say, that they had everything but the experience of receiving the Holy Spirit.

If this were true, then it was not necessary for Christ to die; for the Natural man would have everything that we, as New Creation men and women possess.

But you see that was not true.

"Jesus had to die for our sins according to the Scripture." I Cor. 15:3.

Heb. 9:26, "He had to put sin away by the sacrifice of himself."

You see, there was no ground on which God could remit the trespasses and sins of Natural man, until Christ had suffered as their substitute.

John 6:36, "Jesus said, I am the bread of life, he that cometh to me shall never know hunger and he that believeth on me shall never thirst."

That could not be true until Christ had dealt with the Sin Problem, carried His Blood into the Holy of Holies, His Sacrifice had been accepted, and He sat down at the Right Hand of the Father.

When He declared that we were to eat His Body and drink His Blood, He was referring to the New Blood Covenant.

When we partake of the Lord's Table, we are ratifying that New Covenant between Christ and the Father, of which we are the beneficiaries.

Jesus is the Surety of that New Covenant.

Jesus could not give them the Light of Life, spoken of in John 8:12. "I am the light of the world, he that followeth me shall not walk in the darkness, but shall have the light of life."

Jn. 1:4, "In him was life and that life was the light of men."

It was not until after His Substitutionary Sacrifice that this Scripture could become a reality.

You see the Light of Life is really the Wisdom of God.

In 1 Cor. 1:30 it tells us "But of him are ye in Christ Jesus, who was made unto us wisdom from God, and righteousness, and sanctification, and redemption."

Jesus has been made unto you Wisdom.

That Wisdom is Light.

It is the impartation of God's ability to us.

It is the ability to use knowledge to advantage.

In John 12:35-36, Jesus said, "Yet a little while is the light among you. Walk while ye have the light, that darkness overtake you not: and he that walketh in the darkness knoweth not whither he goeth." "While ye have the light, believe on the light, that ye may become sons of light."

You remember in I John 1:5, it says "And this is the message which we have heard from him and announce unto you, that God is light, and in him is no darkness at all."

The sixth and seventh verses read, "If we say that we have fellowship with him and walk in darkness, we lie, and do not the truth. But if we walk in the light, as he is in the light, we have fellowship one with another and the blood of Jesus, his Son, cleanseth us from all sin."

Here you see the reason for eternal life in the human spirit.

When we come into the relationship of sons of God, it is because we have received eternal life, the nature of the Father.

This could not take place until the great substitution had taken place.

Jesus said to the woman of Samaria in John 4:14, "Whosoever drinketh of the water that I shall give him shall never thirst; but the water that I shall give him shall become in him a well of water springing up unto eternal life."

Jesus could not give that water to any one until He had paid the penalty of their sins.

When men were recreated they could receive the water of Life.

Now notice these facts; He healed their bodies, but they became sick again.

He fed them, but they hungered again.

He clothed them, but they became naked again.

He raised them from the dead, to die again.

He could meet all of the physical needs of men, but He could not change their spiritual condition until He died for them.

He could cast Satan out of their physical bodies, but He had yet to strip Satan of his authority over their spirits.

Col. 2:15: "Having despoiled the principalities and the powers, he made a show of them openly, triumphing over them in it." (Marg.)

You may ask, "but what did Jesus mean when He said, in John 15:5 "I am the vine, ye are the branches: He that abideth in me and I

115

in him, the same beareth much fruit, for apart from me you can do nothing."

Jn. 14:1 through the 17th chapter, is a prophecy and a promise.

It reveals what the disciples were to be, after they were Born Again.

This was written seventy years after the Day of Pentecost, and referred only to those who were Born Again.

The Christ Paul Knew

Paul did not know the Jesus of the Four Gospels with whom Peter and John fellowshipped for three and one-half years.

In II Cor. 5:16 Paul tells us "Wherefore we henceforth know no man after the flesh; even though we knew Christ after the flesh we know him so no more."

This scripture bothered me for a long while. I wondered what Paul meant. Then it opened and I saw that Paul had the same Christ that John had, but John saw Him only with Sense Knowledge eyes.

John had a Sense Knowledge conception of Jesus.

God had given to Paul a Revelation of Jesus.

He did not see the physical Man, he saw the spiritual.

He saw Him as the Substitute.

Paul saw Him made sin on the cross.

He did not see the Man the others saw nailed to the tree.

He saw His Spirit bearing the sins and diseases of the human race.

He saw that Spirit become sin. It was Deity that had been hidden in humanity in that physical body.

To Paul it was always Deity.

He saw Him take man's place, go where man should go, suffer what man should suffer because of the Adamic tragedy.

Paul saw Him when the Supreme Court of the Universe declared that He had paid the penalty of man's transgression and satisfied the claims of Justice.

Paul saw Him justified.

He saw Him as the first born from the dead.

He saw Him when God said "This day have I begotten thee."

In other words Paul saw Him Born Again in the dark regions where He had been suffering the torments of the damned for man.

Now He is not only declared Righteous but He is made Righteous.

Paul saw Jesus become the Master of the dark forces.

"He puts off from himself the principalities and the powers and makes a show of them openly."

He mastered them.

Now He is able to say, "I was dead and behold I am alive forever more, and I have the keys of death and of Hades."

Hebrews 2:14 tells us that, "He paralyzed the death dealing power of Satan." (Roth.)

He broke the bonds of death and left Hades.

He entered into His immortal body.

When He was on the cross and sin touched His body, it immediately became mortal, subject to death.

Now that mortal body has received Immortality.

When Jesus appeared before the disciples, they did not know that He had Immortality. Their eyes were blinded; they only had sense knowledge.

He had died as a man as far as they knew.

He was raised from the dead as a man.

They were mystified, but exceedingly happy over His resurrection.

Some of them had great dreams now of a Jewish nation with Jesus as the king.

You recall in Acts I, before His ascension, the disciples asked Him if He was about to restore the kingdom.

You can catch a glimpse of their political aspirations for they were natural men.

No one knew Him.

Paul was the first person who ever really knew Jesus.

He sees Him ascend with His own blood and enter into the Heavenly Holy of Holies.

He sees the Father accept His blood as the seal of man's eternal redemption.

Paul sees Him go to Paradise with the glad tidings of His finished redemption; cashing the promissory notes of Atonement that had been given from year to year by the High Priest in the earthly Holy of Holies.

The Old Testament saints are redeemed and He takes them to Heaven with Him.

Paul sees all of this.

Then climaxing the wonderful drama of redemption, Paul sees Jesus sit down at the right hand of the Majesty on High as the great High Priest of the New Covenant.

He has given them the New Law of the New Covenant.

The Church is to be the beneficiary of the New Covenant.

There will be two priesthoods of this New Covenant.

One will be the Holy Priesthood, the other is the Royal Priesthood.

The Holy Priesthood will be our fellowship and walk with the Father, it will always be toward Him.

The Royal Priesthood will be to "show forth the excellencies of Him who called us out of darkness into his marvelous life."

It will be a duel priesthood; one part of it will be toward the world and the other part will be toward the body of Christ.

The Pauline Revelation will forever stand as the most marvelous document ever put into print.

There are more than one hundred distinct teachings that no one had ever dreamed of before.

If Paul is simply a literary genius, then he outstrips anything the world has ever known.

All that natural man has been able to do or get has been a product of his five senses.

Paul's ministry was a revelation.

This chapter contains a very simple but valuable truth.

The average preacher does not divide the Word according to his congregation; consequently, many times he delivers a message to the believer that belongs to the unbeliever; or a message that belongs to the adults is given to the babes in Christ.

The message that should be given to babes is often overlooked entirely.

I want in this chapter to show Paul's three men, the natural man without eternal life, the new creation man that has never grown or developed in the divine life, and the believer who has taken advantage of his rights in Christ; and has grown to the point where he can bear fruit to the glory of the Father.

This believer has come to appreciate his righteousness.

He knows that knowledge adds responsibility and he also knows that he has the ability of God to meet this demand.

Chapter XIX

PAUL'S THREE MEN

HE Revelation that God gave to Paul has many startling surprises.

One of them is found in I Cor. 10:32: "Give no occasion of stumbling, either to Jews, or to Greeks or to the church of God."

Here we have God's ethnic divisions of the human race.

The Jew is ever a Jew.

He may become a believer, but he is a Jewish believer.

The Gentile means the heathen world.

Everyone outside of the Christ who is not a Jew is a heathen or Gentile.

The Church, the body of Christ, the New Creation, stands utterly alone.

It is not the professed church, but it is the New Creation.

Then Paul has another division: the Natural man, the Carnal man, and the Spiritual man.

The natural man is the one who has never yet passed out of death into life; he has never been Recreated.

He is spiritually dead, without God and without hope.

The carnal man is the New Creation in Christ who has never developed or grown.

He may stay in that condition through a long life, never developing beyond the babyhood state of the New Creation.

He is governed by his senses, rather than by his spirit.

The spiritual man is the one who has developed in divine things.

His spirit has gained the ascendancy over his intellectual processes, and his spirit has gained the ascendancy over his senses.

God governs him through His Word.

The Natural Man

Let us look carefully at these three men. We will deal first with the natural man.

I Cor. 2:14: "Now the natural man receiveth not the things of the Spirit of God: for they are foolishness unto him; and he cannot know them, because they are spiritually understood."

This natural man is the unspiritual, physical man.

In some places, as in James 3:15 (Mar. Am. Rev.), he is called the demoniacal man, one ruled by Satan.

Romans 8:7: "Because the mind of the flesh (senses) is enmity against God, for it is not subject to the law of God, neither indeed can it be; and they that are in the flesh (senses) cannot please God."

That is the man who lives in his senses.

In the eighth chapter of Romans, wherever the word, "flesh" is translated, it should have been given the real spiritual thought and translated "senses,"

For instance, Romans 8:3: "For what the law could not do, in that it was weak through the senses, God, sending his own son in the likeness of sinful senses and for sin, condemned sin in the senses."

You understand that all the knowledge natural man has, is received by him through the five senses, and that his mind is governed by these senses.

Sense Knowledge is all the knowledge that the world possesses.

We have Revelation Knowledge plus this world knowledge.

It is deeply important that every believer notice the contrast between Sense Knowledge and Revelation Knowledge.

Many of our modern theologians are Sense Knowledge men.

Most of our leaders of the church today are Sense Knowledge men.

They are not spiritually developed, but ruled by the senses.

Many of them repudiate Revelation Knowledge giving it a second place.

This natural man cannot understand the things of the Spirit of God. They are foolishness unto him.

Eph. 2:1-3: "And you did He make alive, when ye were dead through your trespasses and sins, wherein ye once walked according to the course of this world, according to the prince of the powers of the air, of the spirit that now worketh in the sons of disobedience."

Here is the natural man, walking according to the course of this age.

He is walking according to the prince of the authority of the air.

He is being ruled by the spirit that is working in the sons of disobedience.

The next verse says he is doing the desires of the Senses and is by nature a child of wrath.

That is strong language, but it describes the man outside of Christ.

Verse 11 and 12: "Wherefore remember, that once, ye, the Gentiles in the senses, who are called Uncircumcision by that which is called Circumcision, in the senses, made by hands; that ye were at that time separate from Christ, alienated from the commonwealth of Israel, and strangers from the Covenants of the promise, having no hope and without God in the world."

The Gentile has no claim or hold on God today.

He has no legal standing or rights.

I Cor. 1:28: "And the base things of the world, and the things that are despised, did God choose, yea and the things that are not, that He might bring to nought the things that are."

The Centenary translation reveals that the things that are not, represented the slaves of the Roman empire.

They had no standing, no voice, they were just things that were not.

When they became Christians, they had a standing before God.

I Pet. 2:10: "Who in time past were no people, but now are the people of God, who had not obtained mercy, but now have obtained mercy."

The Gentile has no standing. He is a "no people."

With all his boasted culture, ability, and money, he has no voice, no standing with God.

That is a picture of utter spiritual bondage.

It is like a burned forest, absolutely hopeless.

When he says that he is "without God," that means godless.

"Without hope" is hopeless.

Eph. 4:17-19: "This I say therefore, and testify in the Lord, that ye no longer walk as the Gentiles also walk, in the vanity of their mind, being darkened in their understanding, alienated from the life of God, because of the ignorance that is in them, because of the hardening of their heart."

They are walking in the vanity of Sense Knowledge.

If the scholastic world cannot see their photograph here, they will never see it.

They are darkened in their understanding.

They are alienated from the life of God.

They are filled with their own knowledge; that is, ignorance of spiritual things.

Rom. 1:21: "Because that, knowing God, they glorified Him not as God, neither gave thanks; but became vain in their reasonings, and their senseless heart was darkened. Professing themselves to be wise, they became fools."

25th verse: "They refused to have God in their knowledge."

II Cor. 4:4: "In whom the God of this world hath blinded the minds of the unbelieving, that the light of the gospel of the glory of Christ, who is the image of God, should not dawn upon them."

This man's hope is described by the Master in Jn. 14:6.

"I am the way, and the truth, and the life: no one cometh unto the Father, but through me."

Acts 4:12: "And in none other is there salvation: for neither is there any other name under heaven, that is given among men, wherein we must be saved."

There is one Approach and one Name.

That Approach and that Name neglected, despised, or rejected, leaves the man absolutely without hope.

Yet, Redemption belongs to him. Eternal Life is his.

Jn. 3:16: "For God so loved the world, that He gave His only begotten Son, that whosoever believeth on Him should not perish, but have Eternal Life."

Eternal Life is offered to him.

It actually belongs to him if he will take possession of it.

Rom. 3:21-26 declares the lengths to which God went to give man Eternal Life and Righteousness.

These two great blessings belong to man.

He does not have to cry or pray for them.

All he has to do is take them.

They are his as a gift.

Rom. 3:26: "For the showing, I say, of his righteousness at this present season: that he might himself be righteous, and the righteousness of him that hath faith in Jesus."

Rom. 4:25: "Who was delivered up for our trespasses, and was raised for our Justification."

Christ took our place as our substitute and paid the penalty of our transgression.

Rom. 5:1: "Being therefore Justified by faith, we have peace with God through our Lord Jesus Christ."

It belongs to us. It is ours.

9th verse, (Literal trans.): "Much more then, being now Justified by His blood, shall we be saved from the wrath of God through Him. For if while we were enemies, we were reconciled," then every unsaved man has a legal right to Eternal Life if he will take it.

God cannot force this upon him, but if he will accept it, he may have it.

Carnal, or Babes in Christ

The Greek word which is translated "Carnal" has created much comment, and no little confusion among Bible teachers.

Only in later years has the Spirit made this word clear to our minds.

In some scriptures it is translated "Carnal" and in others "fleshly."

It really means the man who is governed by the Senses.

He walks after the order of man.

I Cor. 3:1: "And I, brethern, could not speak unto you as unto spiritual, but as unto carnal, as unto babes in Christ."

He gives his own definition of the Greek word "Sarx." It is a babe, an undeveloped one.

I Cor. 3:2-3: "I fed you with milk, not with meat; for ye were not yet able to bear it: nay, not even now are ye able; for ye are yet carnal; for whereas there is among you jealousy and strife, are ye not carnal, and do ye not walk after the manner of men?"

They were walking just like the world men walked.

They had not yet learned the love law nor the love walk.

For when we begin to walk in love, we stop being jealous; we stop strife, bitterness and backbiting.

All these are signs of undevelopment on the part of the believer.

As long as you are selfish, sensitive, and can be hurt, you are still a babe in Christ.

We need to study very carefully I Cor. 13 with the first epistle of John, going over those great love teachings.

I Cor. 13:5: "Love seeketh not its own." The babes are always saying, "Mother, Jimmy has my cart."

They are quarreling over their own, of which someone has robbed them.

The quarrels in our modern homes, and the divorces, give a picture of the babyhood state of the modern church.

This babyhood condition can be remedied by a study of the Word.

Our Bible Study Course on the plan of Redemption should be studied by every believer; it would lead him out of his babyhood state into full grown manhood and womanhood in Christ.

Ephesians 4:7 is God's commentary on this.

"But unto each one of us was the grace given according to the measure of the gift of Christ."

In this we see each believer has a deposit of grace that will meet every emergency of his life.

Every believer has the same Holy Spirit, the same Eternal Life, the same Love, the same Grace, and the same ability of God.

We have the same matchless Father-God, the same great eternal intercessor, Christ.

There is no reason for any of us to be weak.

There is no reason for us to remain babies when by reason of time we should be developed.

Ephesians 4:11-13: "And He gave some to be apostles; and some, prophets; and some, evangelists; and some, pastors and teachers; for the perfecting of the saints, unto the work of ministering unto the building up of the body of Christ: till we all attain unto the unity of the faith, and of the knowledge of the Son of God, unto a full-grown man, unto the measure of the stature of the fulness of Christ."

What a picture this is of a full-grown believer, of a man rightly dividing the Word, of a man resting quietly in the strength of God.

Ps. 27:1 then becomes a reality.

"Jehovah is my light and my salvation; whom shall I fear? Jehovah is the strength of my life: Of whom shall I be afraid?"

He is your light.

He is your salvation.

He is your physical and mental strength.

You are a conqueror, a victor, an overcomer in Him.

God never planned on your remaining a baby spiritually any more than He planned on your remaining a baby physically and mentally.

Eph. 3:20: "Now unto Him that is able to do exceeding abundantly above all that we ask or think, according to the power that worketh in us."

We have the ability of God in us.

Phil. 4:13: "I can do all things in Him who is my ability, my strength."

There is no place for undevelopment.

Heb. 5:11-14: "Of whom we have many things to say, and hard of interpretation, seeing you have become dull of hearing."

If the believer is not careful, he will become dull of hearing, so that the Word cannot reach him.

"For when by reason of time ye ought to be teachers, ye have need again that someone teach you the rudiments of the first principles of the oracles of God, and are become such as have need of milk, and not of solid food."

Every believer should aspire to be a teacher at least of someone.

"For everyone that partaketh of milk is without experience of the Word of Righteousness; for he is a babe."

Solid food is for full-grown men.

II Tim. 3:7: "Ever learning, and never able to come to the knowledge of the truth."

We see them going to church Sunday after Sunday, ever hearing, ever learning, yet never arriving.

If calamity, sickness, loss of property, or death of loved ones comes, they stand paralyzed and helpless in the presence of the enemy.

They have the resources of God; they have the ability of God; they have His loving Word, but they have never taken advantage of it.

They have never availed themselves of the riches that are theirs.

When the crisis comes, they are unable to take advantage of His ability.

These are children of God who have never developed; they have stayed in their infancy.

Eph. 5:1-2 shows what they could be.

"Be ye therefore imitators of God, as beloved children; and walk in love, even as Christ also loved you. . . . ."

That is their privilege.

That is where they could live.

They do not know the New Covenant Law which is to govern them.

Jn. 13:34-35: "A new commandment I give unto you, that ye love one another; even as I have loved you, that ye also love one another. By this shall all men know that ye are my disciples, if ye have love one for another."

This love is to absolutely govern the heart life of the church.

I Cor. 10:24: "Let no man seek his own, but each his neighbor's good.

When love does not rule, the motives of the life become distorted and the conduct becomes abnormal and the Senses rule the spirit, causing the mind to be brought into bondage to earthly things.

Rom. 12:2 shows that the primal need of this man is to have his mind renewed.

"And be not fashioned according to this age: but be ye transformed by the renewing of your mind, that ye may prove what is the good and acceptable and perfect will of God."

The unrenewed mind is the state of babyhood.

Col. 3:10: "And have put on the new man, that is being renewed unto knowledge after the image of Him that created him."

It is deeply important that the believer's mind be renewed after the image of Jesus.

This can only come as the Spirit guides us into the reality of our Redemption in Christ.

In Jn. 16:13 Jesus said: "Howbeit when He, the Spirit of reality, is come, He shall guide you into all the reality: for He shall not speak from Himself; but what things soever He shall hear, these shall He speak: and He shall declare unto you the things that are to come. He shall glorify me: for He shall take of mine, and shall declare it unto you."

This is the privilege of every believer.

Eph. 4:23 is another exhortation of the Spirit.

"That ye be renewed in the spirit of your mind, and put on the new man, that after God hath been created in Righteousness and holiness of truth."

We must simply learn to know the Father and grow up in the Word until we walk in love.

The Spiritual Man

Eph. 1:3: "Blessed be the God and Father of our Lord Jesus Christ, who hath blessed us with every spiritual blessing in the heavenlies in Christ."

The spiritual man is one who has drunk deeply of the fountain, fed regularly at the table of the Lord, and then has saturated himself in love.

This man has come to know the Father in reality, to know the Lord Jesus in His great ministry at the Right Hand of the Father, and has come to know the blessed intimacy of the Spirit as He is unveiled in the Word.

I Cor. 2:12 is another precious invitation of the Spirit to go into the deep things of God.

"But we received, not the spirit of the world, but the spirit which is from God; that we might know the things that were freely given to us of God."

The spiritual man is one in whom the Word has gained the ascendancy over his mind and body.

It has brought him into harmony with the will of the Father for this age.

The things which have been freely given to us of God are the things which we speak not in the words which man's wisdom teaches, but which the Spirit teaches.

It is an unveiling of spiritual things by the aid and energy of God Himself.

Col. 1:12 (Free translation): "Giving thanks unto the Father, who has given us the ability to enjoy our share of the inheritance of the saints in light."

God is our ability.

That ability reveals itself in unveiling the treasures of grace that belong to us now.

Jesus said in Acts 1:8: "Ye shall receive power, when the Holy Spirit is come upon you."

That word "power" is "ability." You have ability to witness, ability to know and do the will of the Father, and ability to know how to use the Name of Jesus and how to enter into all the fulness of our inheritance in Christ.

The Holy Spirit is your ability.

Col. 1:13-14: "Who delivered us out of the authority of darkness, and translated us into the kingdom of the Son of His love; in whom we have our redemption, the remission of our sins."

You have been delivered out of Satan's authority.

You have been translated into the kingdom of the Son of His love.

You are in the place of His protection and care.

You are in the place where you feed upon the bread of the Mighty.

The manna of heaven is in this living Word.

As you feed upon it, you will grow up spiritually into the image and the stature of the Son of God.

Prayer will no longer be groaning and struggling, or a plea always for faith and forgiveness.

It will be a holy, sweet intimacy.

You will come into the presence of your Father on the ground of your rights.

The spiritual man knows that he is the Righteousness of God.

He knows that Righteousness means the ability to stand in the Father's presence as though sin had never been.

Righteousness gives him the sense of equality and of relationship with the Father.

He is a son, and He has a son's place.

He takes a son's privileges and enjoys them.

He assumes a son's responsibilities and rises to the level of his opportunities.

He is not a beggar.

He is not just a sinner who has been forgiven.

He is a New Creation created in Christ Jesus.

II Cor. 5:17 is the background of his life.

"Wherefore if any man is in Christ, there is a new creation: the old things are passed away; behold, they are become new. And all these things are of God, who reconciled us to Himself through Christ."

We are in the family.

We are sons and daughters.

The old things of weakness and failure, of doubt and fear, have passed into forgetfulness.

We take our place and enjoy our rights.

We know what the lordship of love means.

We whisper, "The Lord is my Shepherd. I do not want.

"Today He leads me beside the green pastures and the waters of gentle stillness.

"He restores my soul and makes me perfectly normal.

"He takes away the sense of weakness and failure.

"He leads me down the paths of Righteousness where I use His Name and walk with Him.

"I have no sense of guilt or sin. I am in the Beloved.

"The great Spirit who raised Jesus from the dead makes His home in my body."

He is the Righteousness of God

Of all the wealth and riches of Grace that were revealed in Christ, nothing equals the fact of our becoming, through the New Birth, the Righteousness of God.

This opens the very doors of heaven.

This permits access into the Holy of Holies.

This is our entry into the very presence of the Father with joy that is unspeakable and full of glory.

We are now not only sons and daughters, but we are the Righteousness of God in Him.

II Cor. 5:21: "Him who knew no sin, God made to become sin; that we might become the Righteousness of God in Him."

We have come into this Righteousness realm.

We are now capable of the sweetest, fullest fellowship with the Father.

I Cor. 1:9 tells us that He has called us into fellowship with his Son.

This is the highest honor that the Father can bestow upon us.

There is no remembrance of what we have been.

There is only the fact of what we are.

We are sons of God with a standing that God Himself has given us, with a relationship that His nature has given us, with privileges that love alone could vouchsafe.

We have passed out of the babyhood state into manhood's full rights and privileges.

Disease and weakness can no longer feed upon our vitality and sap us of our spiritual virility.

We know that Isaiah 53:3-4 is true.

"Surely He hath borne our sicknesses and carried our diseases, and we have come to esteem Him as the one who was stricken, smitten of God and afflicted. He was wounded for our transgressions, bruised for our iniquities; the chastisement of our peace was upon Him, and with His stripes we are healed."

This belongs to the one who has come to enjoy the fruits of Righteousness.

Now instead of praying for healing, you simply look up and say, "Father, I thank thee that by His stripes I am now healed.

"My spirit is free from sin and disease.

"There is therefore now no condemnation to me, because I am in Christ Jesus where no disease has a right to reign."

It makes no difference what the disease is, by His stripes you are. There is no "may be" about it.

There is no problem of faith about it.

You are in the family.

It took faith to get into the family but now you are in it and all that the family affords, is yours.

You can say, "I thank thee that through Jesus Christ, I am perfectly free:

"By His stripes I am healed.

"I know that my God does supply every need of mine, physical, mental, and spiritual.

"Satan's dominion over me is ended.

"Thank God, at last I am free."

≡Ⅱ≡Ⅱ≡Ⅱ≡Ⅱ≡Ⅱ≡Ⅱ≡Ⅱ≡Ⅱ≡Ⅱ≡Ⅱ≡Ⅱ≡Ⅱ≡Ⅱ≡Ⅱ≡Ⅱ≡Ⅲ

I suppose there has always been a body of Judeisers, as Paul called them, who are seeking to get under the First Covenant and keep its Law.

They are ignorant of what the New Covenant has granted them.

They do not know that in this New Covenant there is a Law that covers everything that the Mosaic Law covered.

They do not understand that the New Creation folk cannot live under the Mosaic Law; nor can the Old Creation folk live under the New Covenant Law.

The New Covenant belongs to the New Creation folk, the sons and daughters of God.

The Abrahamic Covenant belongs to the Old Covenant folk, the servants of Jehovah.

The Old Covenant was given only to the sons of Abraham, it belonged to Israel, and Israel alone.

The New Covenant is not given to the world; it is given to the New Creation and to the New Creation only.

The Old Covenant with its Law can only be kept in Palestine.

It requires a Priesthood to make a yearly Atonement because it is a Law of sin and of death.

The New Covenant is a Law of Righteousness and of Life.

≡Ⅱ≡Ⅱ≡Ⅱ≡Ⅱ≡Ⅱ≡Ⅱ≡Ⅱ≡Ⅱ≡Ⅱ≡Ⅱ≡Ⅱ≡Ⅱ≡Ⅱ≡Ⅱ≡Ⅱ≡Ⅲ

Chapter XX

IS THE CHURCH UNDER THE MOSAIC LAW?

THERE has never been a clear-cut distinction in the mind of the church between the Abrahamic Covenant, and the New Covenant in the blood of Christ.

When God cut the Covenant with Abraham, it was to the end that there might come into being a New Nation, a people in Covenant relationship with God; and out of this Covenant people should come the Redeemer of the human race.

Abraham's descendants, during a famine, migrated to Egypt and became a nation of about four million people. They were led out of captivity, across the Red Sea and started on their journey toward the promised land. All they had was the memory of a Covenant and the seal of circumcision. They had no Law and no Priesthood.

They had no religious teaching. When they came out of Egypt, a nation of slaves, God gave them the law of the Covenant. With this Law, He gave them the Priesthood, Sacrifices and the Offerings. Then He gave an interpretation of the Law which is recorded in Numbers and Deuteronomy.

The book of Leviticus had to do largely with the Offerings and Priesthood, the Sacrifices, and the Holy Days. This Law and the ceremony and Priesthood were given to the Israelites and to the Israelites only.

No Gentile was under these laws nor had any part in the covenant blessings.

While Israel kept the Covenant and walked in the Law, there was no sickness among them, nor could the nations conquer them.

David's blood-covenant warriors give us a history of supermen that staggers the imagination.

The book of Daniel gives us a picture of God's Covenant people in captivity, menaced by heathenism and heathen religions; which would have utterly destroyed them as a nation had not God, through Daniel and his three friends, saved Israel from the worshipping of idols.

The miracle of Daniel's dream and interpretation, the three Hebrew children being thrown into the fiery furnace, Daniel's deliverance from the Lion's den, and the translation of the writing on the wall, shook not only the heathen nation to its foundation, but emancipated Israel from the heathen gods.

They never went back to serving heathen gods again, though they were hopelessly entangled in a foreign captivity.

When Israel walked in the Covenant, neither sickness nor poverty was among them. It was not given to the heathens. It was given only to the Covenant people, the sons of Abraham.

During Jesus' ministry, He expounded the Law and called Israel back to the Covenant. Jesus did not put the heathen nations under the Law.

No one was under the Law in the days of Christ, but the Jews.

Jesus's coming was for the fulfillment of the Abrahamic Covenant.

When He fulfilled that Covenant, the Law automatically stopped functioning.

The Priesthood ceased to minister before Jehovah; the sacrifices no longer had any meaning.

Jesus had fulfilled the Abrahamic Covenant. It was folded up as a worn out garment and laid aside.

Jesus introduced a New Covenant, a New Law, with a new Priesthood, a new Sacrifice and a new People.

The first people were born of circumcized parentage. This second people are born of the Spirit and instead of circumcision of the body, they have the Circumcision of the heart, or, the New Birth.

With this New Creation people came the new Law that Jesus gave in Jn. 13:34-35. "A new commandment I give unto you, that ye love one another; even as I have loved you, that ye also love one another. By this shall all men know that ye are my disciples, if ye have love one to another."

This is the Law that is to govern this New Creation, this New Covenant people.

Heb. 8:1-2 tells us that Jesus is the High Priest of this New Covenant.

When the veil of the Temple was rent in two from top to bottom as recorded in Matt. 27:50-51, it was the end of the earthly Holy of Holies. It no longer functions.

The new Holy of Holies is in Heaven. Jesus is our High Priest.

I Pet. 2:1-9 tells us of the two Priesthoods on earth now; the Holy Priesthood that offers up sacrifices of worship and love, and the Royal Priesthood that shows forth the excellence of Him who called us out of darkness into light.

One is our holy, private ministry of love; the other is the public ministry of the Word.

The problem that confronts the church now is, what is its relationship to the Old Covenant?

It has no relationship.

No Gentile was ever under the Old Covenant or could get under it, except by circumcision and obedience to a special ritual.

No Jew or Israelite can get into the Old Covenant now for it has been set aside and replaced by a New Covenant.

Is the church now to keep the Ten Commandments?

No, the Ten Commandments were given to unrecreated men. They do not fit into a believer's life.

If we are New Creations, we can obey the new law of the New Covenant, which covers everything that was in the law of the First Covenant.

I Cor. 10:32 gives us God's division of the human race: the Jew, the Gentile, and the Church of God.

The Gentile represents all the people who have not been Born Again.

The Church represents only those who have become New Creations, not the great body of denominationalism, the professing Christians who have not been Born Again.

We have three classes: the Jew, the unsaved world, and the New Creation. The world is under neither the Jewish law, or the New Covenant law. They are outside.

I Pet. 2:10 declares that they are a "no people." They have no standing. God does not recognize them. There is only one sin for which they will be judged: that is the rejection of the Lord Jesus. They are not under the teaching of Jesus in the four Gospels. We have tried to legislate them there. The church has tried to make laws that would govern the unsaved world, and put them under bondage to the Bible, but they have no relation to it.

Only the sons and daughters of God are under obligation to the New Covenant. Take the subject of marriage as an illustration. Moses laid down the law in regard to marriage. Jesus' interpretation of that law lifts it to its real place in the mind of Jehovah.

But that law does not govern the unsaved world nor the church. The laws of marriage and divorce are given to us in God's Revelation of the church in Paul's Epistles.

I Cor. 7: shows us clearly that two believers have no right to a divorce and remarriage. If they are separated, they should come back together again rather than to be divorced and remarry, but to the mixed marriage, he said, "That if the unsaved husband is content to live with a Christian wife, let her not seek a divorce for she may be able to lead him to Christ." But if he leaves her, she is not under bondage to the marriage vows. That leaves the Christian free to marry again.

He forbids the marriage of Christians with unbelievers.

They are not to be unequally yoked together, but if they are in that condition, the believer is to remain and seek to lead the other to Christ.

The church could not be under the Law.

The early church gave us distinct teaching in regard to the church's relationship to the Law. "Not to put a yoke upon the neck of Gentile believers, that we Jews cannot bear."

Acts 15:10-11: "But we believe that we shall be saved through the grace of the Lord Jesus, in like manner as they."

There had been much discussion among the Gentile Christians

and the Jewish Christians as to whether or not they were under the Mosaic Law. They sent Paul and Barnabas to Jerusalem and after much discussion, we hear them say, "But we believe that we shall be saved through the grace of the Lord Jesus, in like manner as they."

Then James, the half brother of Jesus, who was at the head of the church in Jerusalem says this: "Wherefore my judgment is, that we trouble not them that from among the Gentiles turn to God; but that we write unto them, that they abstain from the pollutions of idols, and from fornication, and from what is strangled, and from blood.

"For Moses from generations of old hath in every city them that preach him, being read in the synagogues every Sabbath. For it seemed good to the Holy Spirit, and to us, to lay upon you no greater burden than these necessary things."

There is not one word about keeping the Sabbath or keeping the Law. The Law, with its Sabbaths and all its Sacrifices belonged to the old order, the Old Covenant.

You cannot separate the Mosaic Ten Commandments from the Mosaic Sacrifice and Offerings. They illustrate to us God's attitude and teaching to natural men, under the Law.

There were no New Creations, no one was Born Again until the day of Pentecost. "But," you say, "Isn't faith in Jesus the means of salvation?" Yes, but it is faith in His Resurrection.

Rom. 10:9-10: "Because if thou shalt confess with thy mouth Jesus as Lord, and shalt believe in thy heart that God raised Him from the dead, thou shalt be saved."

The faith of the disciples until the day of Pentecost, and the faith of the Jews around Jesus was not faith in his Substitutionary Sacrifice and in His Resurrection. It was faith in His ability to raise the dead, and heal the sick.

Their faith was based upon Sense evidence. Our faith is based upon the Word of God. We believe that He died for our sins according to scripture and that He was raised again for our Justification.

They believed that He was the prophet. Some believed that He was the Son of God, but they did not believe that He had died for them, and was going to rise again for their Justification.

That was not believed or understood by anyone. There was not a soul that accepted the fact of His Resurrection until Sense evidence had absolutely satisfied them. If one person could have been Born Again before Christ died and rose again and the Holy Spirit came, then every person could have been Born Again, because, all are under sin.

All are condemned for one thing.

They are spiritually dead.

The thing that the world needs is not only forgiveness of sins, but eternal life, and a New Creation.

Let it be fully understood that the forgiveness of sins will not save a sinner today. He must have something more than forgiveness, for if all that God did was to forgive him his sins, he would go on living in sin; for he could not help it. Sin is in man's spirit, it is his spirit that is recreated.

He needs to be born again.

He needs to be born from above.

He needs eternal life.

Most of the people who attempt to put themselves under the Law today, do not believe in the New Creation. They believe that the New Birth comes at the second coming of Jesus; that the believers who have died, are asleep in the grave, and when they are raised, they will be recreated.

If they are not recreated now, then they are simply unsaved men and women, and being unsaved, they cannot understand or know the Word.

I Cor. 2:14: "Now the natural man understandeth not the things of the spirit of God: for they are foolishness unto him: and he cannot know them, because they are spiritually understood." These people who deny the New Birth, cannot understand the Word of God.

Consequently, they try to put themselves under the Old Covenant. James tells us that even the Jews could not keep that and be justified. These folks are attempting to justify themselves by keeping the Law.

Romans 7:1-2: "Or are ye ignorant, brethren (for I speak to men who know the law), that the law hath dominion over a man for so long time as he liveth? For the woman that hath a husband is bound by law to the husband while he liveth; but if the husband die, she is discharged from the law of the husband." He is not speaking of a ceremonial law, but the Law of the Old Covenant.

He is talking here to Jews, and He is showing them that when Jesus died on the cross, every Jew died in Christ to the Law. When Christ was raised from the dead, the Law was fulfilled and set aside. Now the Jew can marry Jesus and not be an adulterer. But, if a man is keeping the Law and trying to marry Jesus, then he has two husbands, and that is adultery.

In other words, the Law was fulfilled and set aside, so now the Jew is free to accept Christ as Savior.

The same thing is true in Gal. 4:24-25. The Old Covenant was Sinai. "These two women are two Covenants; one from Mount Sinai, bearing children unto bondage, which is Hagar. Now this Hagar is Mount Sinai in Arabia and answereth to the Jerusalem that now is: for she is in bondage with her children."

Gal. 4:28-31: "Now we, brethren, as Isaac was, are children of promise. But as then he that was born after the flesh persecuted him that was born after the Spirit, so also it is now. Howbeit what saith the scripture? Cast out the handmaid and her son: for the son of the handmaid shall not inherit with the son of the freewoman. Wherefore, brethren, we are not children of a handmaid, but of the freewoman."

He means that the Law and the First Covenant have been cast out as Hagar was cast out with Ishmael and had no right to inherit with Isaac. We are the Isaac, the New Creation.

We are not under the Law. We are not subject to the Law. We are free.

Gal. 3:21: "Is the law then against the promises of God? God forbid: for if there had been a law given which could make alive, verily Righteousness would have been of the law." The promise of God was for a New Creation.

"But the scripture shut up all things under sin, that the promise by faith in Jesus Christ might be given to them that believe."

The law could not give Righteousness, nor Eternal Life. The finished work of Christ gives to us Eternal Life and Righteousness.

Verses 23-24: "But before faith came, we (the Jews) were kept inward under the law, shut up unto the faith which should afterwards be revealed. So that the law is become our tutor until Christ."

The Law had been the Jew's tutor until Christ, that they (Jews) might be Justified on the ground of faith.

25th verse: "But now that faith is come, we are no longer under a tutor."

The reason that the modern Sabbatarian is so zealous is that he is trying to save himself by keeping the Law of the Sabbath. He ignores the finished work of Christ. He knows nothing about it.

Every man or woman who is attempting to keep the Law, unless he has been Born Again previously, has not been Born Again.

The evangelistic meetings of Sabbatarians are not for the purpose of saving souls, but for proselytizing professed Christians, and getting unsaved men and women to keep the Mosaic Law.

Gal 3:11: "Now that no man is Justified by the law before God, is evident: for, The righteous shall live by faith."

The Law was not of faith but of works. The Law is condemnation. Faith in Jesus Christ means faith in the work that He wrought on our behalf. We do not have to do anything but accept Him as our Saviour.

Upon the Gentiles now has come the blessing of Abraham in Christ Jesus.

We have received the promise of the Spirit on the ground of faith.

Our modern church is slowly leaving the faith realm for the works realm.

Most of our evangelistic preaching is of works. We tell what the people must do in order to be saved.

There is only one thing that they must do: that is to believe on the Lord Jesus Christ.

Our Redemption has been completed; the work is finished. All they have to do is to accept it as theirs.

Galatians 5:1: Paul gives the great warning. "For freedom did Christ set us free; stand fast therefore, and be not entangled again in a yoke of bondage."

Christ has set you free from the Abrahamic Covenant and the Mosaic Law and its rituals. (He is talking to Jews) He is not talking to Gentiles as they were never under the Mosaic Law or the Abrahamic Covenant.

Galatians 4:3: "So we (Jews) also, when we were children, were held in bondage under the rudiments of the world: but when the fulness of the time came, God sent forth His Son, born of a woman, born under the law, that He might redeem them that were under the law, that we might receive the adoption of sons. And because ye are sons, God sent forth the Spirit of his Son into our hearts, crying, Abba, Father."

Notice the next verse, "So that thou art no longer a bondservant, but a son."

Abraham's children were the servants of God. They were never anything higher than that. The church is called the children of God. The Gentiles are heathens, outside of God.

The Abrahamic Covenant gave the Jew Covenant rights.

The New Creation gives the believer a son's place.

The Jews were never anything but servants.

Now to the Jews who accept Christ, he says: "So thou art no longer a servant, but a son; and if a son, then an heir through God."

The Gentile has no claim on God. He is outside. The Jew had a standing. He was a Covenant man.

Jesus came and fulfilled the Covenant, made it possible for the Jew to become a son.

The moment he becomes a son, he calls God his Father. He is no longer under the First Covenant. He is in the New Covenant in Christ Jesus.

The Gentile today who attempts to put himself under the Law is attempting a fruitless thing.

The Law has been fulfilled and set aside with the Covenant to which it belonged.

He is ignoring the finished work of Christ and is attempting to save himself by keeping the Jewish Sabbath which was fulfilled and laid aside.

≡ǁ

This is the Genesis of the New Covenant.

It is what Jesus began to do and to teach in the first thirty-five years of the church.

They did not have the written Word as we have it today.

None of the four gospels had been written; yet everything that the Father had done for us in Christ had been enjoyed.

One day I counted forty-two different New Creation facts that came into being during that period. Since then I have come to know that there are more than one hundred things just as startlingly new as when God said, "Let there be vegetation in the world."

These new facts are not mentioned in the book of Acts; they are mentioned in the Epistles, but they are practiced in the book of Acts.

The omission of these things in Acts is more startling than the things that are mentioned.

For instance, Luke wrote the book of Acts. Luke was led to Christ by Paul.

He traveled with him fifteen to eighteen years.

He knew the Pauline revelation, yet he did not mention one single truth that is given to us in Paul's Epistles.

This proves that God governed the writing of that Book.

The same is illustrated in the Gospels.

Read this chapter prayerfully.

Study the book of Acts from this new angle.

≡ǁ

Chapter XXI

SOME FACTS ABOUT THE BOOK OF ACTS

CTS WAS written by Luke in 65 A.D. He was the companion of Paul for about eighteen years and was evidently led to Christ by him.

He knew the Pauline Revelation without any doubt, and yet when he wrote the gospel of Luke, you can't see a mark of the Pauline Revelation in it.

The same thing is true of the Book of Acts.

That drives one to this conclusion, that the men who wrote our New Testament did not write their philosophy, their opinions, or the opinions of others. Neither did they write their convictions.

They wrote as the Holy Spirit gave them the Word.

The Book of Acts is really the Genesis of the New Covenant.

It is the book of the beginning of everything connected with the New Covenant.

It is the beginning of the New Redemption, a Spiritual Redemption.

It is Redemption from Satan.

Ephesians 1:7 gives us the fact of it. "In whom we have our redemption through his blood, the remission of our trespasses and it is according to the riches of his grace."

Or in Colossians 1:13-14: "Who delivered us out of the authority of darkness, and translated us into the kingdom of the Son of his love in whom we have our redemption, the remission of our sins.

Israel had had redemption out of Egypt in the sense realm. But this Redemption was out of the hand of Satan who had held man through the ages in his thrall. It was in the spirit realm.

It was the Beginning of the New Covenant in His Blood

Matthew 26:26-29: "And as they were eating, Jesus took bread, and blessed, and brake it; and he gave to the disciples, and said, Take, eat; this is my body. And he took a cup, and gave thanks, and gave to them, saying, Drink ye all of it; for this is my blood of the new covenant, which is poured out for many unto remission of sins. But I say unto you, I shall not drink henceforth of this fruit of the vine, until that day when I drink it new with you in my Father's kingdom."

You notice "For this is my blood of the New Covenant which is poured out for many unto the remission of sins."

The Abrahamic Covenant had been between Abraham and Jehovah.

It had been sealed with the blood of Jehovah and of Abraham.

But this Covenant is sealed by the blood (or life) of Deity and humanity united in the Man, Jesus; between the Father and Jesus.

The Abrahamic Covenant gave to Israel its home, Palestine.

It gave them what was known as the Mosaic Law, the Priesthood, the atonement, the sacrifices.

These had all been annulled when Jesus said, "It is finished," on the cross, and the veil of the temple had been rent from top to bottom.

God shows by that act, that the Covenant was ended and that the New Covenant, that Jesus had spoken of, was to come into being at once.

The Old Covenant had been with natural man.

This New Covenant is to have a New Creation man.

The other Covenant had servants. This Covenant has sons.

Ephesians 2:10: "For we are his workmanship, created in Christ Jesus for good works, which God afore prepared that we should walk in them."

II Cor. 5:17: "Wherefore if any man is in Christ, he is a new creature: the old things are passed away; behold, they are become new. But all these things are of God."

This is a new type of humanity.

God has given them His own nature, eternal life, thus it was the beginning of man with eternal life, the nature of God.

There is no doubt but what he could have had this nature in the Garden of Eden if he had eaten of the tree of life instead of the tree of the knowledge of good and evil.

It was the beginning of the Family of God.

It must have been a thrilling hour in Heaven when the first children were born. Acts 2:1-4.

Romans 8:14-17: "For as many as are led by the Spirit of God, these are the sons of God. For ye received not the spirit of bondage again unto fear; but ye received the spirit of adoption, whereby we cry, Abba, Father. The Spirit himself beareth witness with our spirit, that we are children of God: and if children, then heirs; heirs of God, and joint-heirs with Christ; if so be that we suffer with Him, that we may be also glorified with him."

It was the beginning of God as a Father.

Jesus introduced Him as a Father God in His public ministry, but so far as we know, He had never had a child born in this new way until Jesus was born of the spirit, before He rose from the dead.

Colossians 1:18: "And he is the head of the body, the church: who is the beginning, the first born from the dead that in all things he might have the preeminence."

It was the beginning of the Remission of Sins.

Under the First Covenant, they had a scape-goat that bore away sins in type.

Jesus had put sin away by the sacrifice of Himself.

John the Baptist said, "Behold the Lamb of God that beareth away the sin of the world."

And on the ground of that, when a man is born again, he receives a remission of all the things that he ever did while he was in the sin life..

Now he comes into the family of God.

You see it was really the beginning of that marvelous ministry of Christ at the Right Hand of the Father.

He is the new High Priest who has entered into the Heavenly Holy of Holies with His own blood making an eternal redemption for us.

Then He sits down at the Right Hand of the Father.

He is now the Mediator of this New Covenant.

No man can reach the Father but through Him.

John 14:6: "Jesus saith unto him, I am the way, and the truth, and the life: no one cometh unto the Father, but by me."

As soon as they have reached the Father, then He becomes their Intercessor.

Hebrews 7:25: "Wherefore also he is able to save to the uttermost them that draw near unto God through him, seeing he ever liveth to make intercession for them."

He is there before the Throne always to intercede for the sons and daughters of this wonderful family of God.

Not only is He the Mediator and Intercessor, but He is their Advocate and family Lawyer.

"I write unto you little children that ye sin not, but if ye sin, ye have an Advocate with the Father, Jesus Christ the Righteous." (I John 2:1.)

He is not only the family Lawyer, but Hebrews 7:22 declares that He is the Surety of the New Covenant.

Just as Jehovah was the Surety of the Old Covenant, Jesus has assumed that office in the New Covenant.

He is back of every promise from Matthew 1: to Revelation 22:

Not only is He back of it, but the Throne is back of it, the Father is back of it.

No word from God can ever be defaulted.

He holds another office that to me is the most priceless.

He is the Lord of the New Covenant.

Lord means bread provider, care-taker and protector.

He is everything that the heart could crave.

It was the Beginning of Fellowship with the Father.

This fellowship is the most beautiful thing connected with Christianity.

All through the ages man has craved fellowship with Heaven, but there was no ground for it.

Man's nature was enmity with God.

"It was not subject to the law of God, neither indeed could it be." (Romans 8:7.)

You see the hope of marriage is fellowship.

The hope of human organizations basically is fellowship.

It is the cream of relationship.

When we sin, we break fellowship.

We mar, but do not break our relationship.

Only God can break that.

The secret of knowing the Bible, of understanding it, is living in fellowship with the Author.

When we break fellowship, we go into darkness.

The Word no longer opens to us.

"But if we walk in the light as He is in the light, we have fellowship one with another, and the blood of Jesus Christ his Son cleanseth us from all sin." (I John 1:7.)

Another marvelous beginning was the use of Jesus' name.

Jesus had given them a legal right, really the power of attorney to use His Name.

Mark 16:17: "And these signs shall accompany them that believe: in my name shall they cast out demons; they shall speak with new tongues."

John 14:13-14: "And whatsoever ye shall ask in my name, that will I do, that the Father may be glorified in the Son. If ye shall ask anything in my name, that will I do."

Or "in my name ye shall cast out demons and lay hands on the sick."

Mighty things were to be done in the Name of Jesus.

This is a lost truth to the church (Read my book "The Wonderful Name of Jesus.")

The beginning of the Indwelling One was the most remarkable promise made by Jesus.

John 14:17: "Even the Spirit of truth: whom the world cannot receive; for it beholdeth him not, neither knoweth him: ye know him; for he abideth with you, and shall be in you."

He speaks of the Holy Spirit and He says he is with you now.

John 16:13: "But when he, the Spirit of Truth, is come, he shall guide you into all the truth: for he shall not speak from himself; but what things soever he shall hear, these shall he speak; and he shall declare unto you the things that are to come."

He will be in you, make His home in you.

On the Day of Pentecost the Holy Spirit came and filled the Upper Room where the disciples were seated.

As He immersed them, He recreated them.

A tongue of fire sat upon the brow of each, indicating that the message was going to be the spoken Word indwelt by God Himself, a resistless message.

And then the Holy Spirit entered the bodies of these New Creation men and women.

They had been made New Creations.

He moved into His temple.

He had moved out of the old temple when the veil was rent.

Now He moved into these recreated men and women.

He was going to live in them.

He was going to make real in them all that He had done for them in Christ.

Then He began to speak to them in unknown tongues, as the Spirit gave them utterance.

That was the Birth and the Beginning of the New Covenant People.

I want you to note this carefully, that these New Covenant people were to be indwelt, lived in by God.

And you will notice this fact, that they were born again before they were indwelt.

The Holy Spirit gave them eternal life first, made them New Creations.

Then He entered them in order that He might build into them the very characteristics of Jesus, the Son of God.

Under the First Covenant, the Holy Spirit came upon men and He spoke through them, or inspired them to write the Old Testament and perform miracles, but as soon as the work was finished, He left them.

He did not change their nature.

They were the same men after they had wrought these miracles as they were before.

It may have left some sweet influence over them, but they were natural men.

Now He made them spiritual men, Recreated men, and He indwelt them.

It was the Beginning of the Grace of God to all Men.

Matthew 28:19-20: "Go ye therefore, and make disciples of all the nations, baptizing them into the name of the Father and of the Son and of the Holy Ghost: teaching them to observe all things whatsoever I commanded you: and lo, I am with you always, even unto the end of the world."

They were to make students of all people.

That means more than converts.

They were not only to lead a man to accept Christ, but they were to teach them the things of Christ.

It was the beginning of the miracle age among all people.

Even the New Birth was a miracle.

Every answered prayer was a miracle.

Every New Creation was a miracle life living in the sense ruled world.

It was the beginning of Man's receiving eternal life.

We have mentioned this before, but we want to elaborate on it now.

John 6:47: "I say unto you, He that believeth hath eternal life."

There are two Greek words translated life.

One is Zoe, eternal life, and the other is Psuche, natural life.

God gave to natural man a Law and told him to keep it, under the First Covenant.

Now He gives man a New Law and gives him the nature to obey it.

Eternal life has given to man all that is best in our civilization.

The backward nations of the world are backward because they do not have eternal life.

Whenever a nation has enough people who have eternal life, it becomes a civilized country.

It is well for us to note this fact, that the Renaissance of Germany and England and the Scandinavian countries did not begin until after the Lutheran revival.

That should make every thinking man ask a question. "What was in that Lutheran revival that gave to us a printing press and all the other inventions that have come to us in the last four hundred years?

It was the creative ability of God that came into the spirit of man.

Understand this fact, that the reasoning faculties are not creative.

The great philosophers have not been creative.

They may have discovered a few laws of nature that would imply a creative element in it.

It was simply that they discovered some facts that had been overlooked by others.

When a man creates a printing press and the thousands upon thousands of machines that have been created, that is something that natural human reason cannot produce.

The Mohammedans have never invented or created anything.

Only the people who have received eternal life in the New Birth have been creative people.

If you study carefully, you will find that there are over forty beginnings in connection with the New Covenant that took place on the Day of Pentecost in the Upper Room.

It was the beginning of Sonship.

Israelites were the servants of God. No one had ever intelligently called God, Father. No one had ever recognized God as a Father.

They feared Him.

They did not love Him.

They obeyed Him as a servant, as a slave. If they did not obey Him, they were punished.

There was a Law with a penalty for breaking it.

Now they are born into His family.

Everyone of them in that Upper Room was a member of this new family of which Jesus was the Lord and Head.

"Beloved, now are we the sons of God, and it does not yet appear what we shall be." (I John 3:2.)

And you notice this fact, that the moment men recognized their sonship rights and their son place in the family, life became different.

There came a new terminology about God.

You could hear men call Him, "My Father."

He was the sinner's God, but He is our Father.

I love to call Him, "My Father God."

He always had a father-heart. Men came into being in answer to that primordial cry in the heart of the Creator.

Can't you see how it solves every problem of your life if He is your Father?

You would not think of asking Him as a Father to give you faith.

But you could if He is only God.

If He is your Father, all you need to do is to become acquainted with Him.

Cultivate a son consciousness.

I remember when I first began to think of Him as my own Father.

I had been in the ministry quite a number of years, but I never read a book that majored the Father fact.

The moment that one begins to realize that the great God of the Universe is his own Father, and that he is the Father's child, and that he has a son's place in the Father's heart, he has a son's rights and responsibilities, life is different.

When this truth first came to my heart, I was thrilled through and through.

He was no longer God. He was my own Father.

And then I began to remember scriptures.

The Spirit brought one after another to me.

John 14:23: "If a man love me, he will keep my word: and my Father will love him, and we will come unto him, and make our abode with him."

I never realized it meant that He would actually live with me.

The "Lo, I am with you always," had been just a figure of speech.

Now it became a reality.

And I remember when Jesus said, "When He the spirit of reality is come, He will guide you into all reality."

And He began to guide me into the reality of sonship.

He had never been very real in my life.

And I had never understood John 16:15: "All things whatsoever the Father hath are mine: therefore said I, that he taketh of mine, and shall declare it unto you."

Now I can understand for the first time the oneness of Jesus and the Father when He said, "All that the Father has is mine."

Then I knew all that the Father had was mine, too.

Just as the son says, "That is our farm," speaking of his father's farm.

The Father and the Son are one.

It is that family oneness, that vital oneness between the Father and His child.

And the Spirit now began to lead me into the reality of my oneness with Jesus and with the Father.

The prayer of Jesus in the seventeenth chapter of John then began to be a reality.

John 17:21: "That they may be one even as thou, Father, art in me and I in thee: that they also may be in us."

We are to be made one with the Father and Jesus.

The Father's interests, the Father's work, the Father's word is to be one with me.

When Jesus said: "He hath not left me alone, He is always with me," I could take that as my own.

When Jesus said: "I know my Father," then I knew that I might become acquainted with my Father.

For the Spirit of reality was going to guide me into the reality of this sonship.

Can't you see that this belongs to every one of us? That it is the end of the age-old fight for faith?

Why, faith becomes as normal and natural as it is in a beautiful family.

Those children are not faith conscious. They are love conscious. They are father conscious. They are son conscious.

You can understand now the vital need of the heart's consciousness of this holy relationship.

It was the beginning of people going to Heaven.

Up to this time men had gone to paradise when they died.

Now John 14:1-6 becomes the new slogan of the heart.

"Let not your heart be troubled: ye believe in God, believe also in me. In my Father's house are many mansions; if it were not so, I would have told you; for I go to prepare a place for you. And if I go and prepare a place for you, I come again, and will receive you unto myself; that where I am there ye may be also, And whither I go, ye know the way. Thomas saith unto him, Lord we know not whither thou goest; how know we the way? Jesus saith unto him, I am the way, and the truth, and the life: no one cometh unto the Father, but by me."

148

Notice "in my Father's house."

Now our hearts can understand it.

In my Father's home there are many dwelling places. There is plenty of room for me.

Jesus said: "I go to prepare a place for you."

That place will be presided over by the Father.

It will be a love home for the children of love.

I am sure we are going to know each other.

We are going to meet those who have passed on before us.

What a family reunion!

If the heart can only take this truth in, it will rob life of its terror.

For the real terror of life is what happens after death.

But Jesus brought a new conception of heaven.

No human religion has a heaven home or a heaven faith but Christianity.

There is no one truth that Jesus brought that has given greater joy to the human heart than His heaven teaching.

At the very beginning of His public ministry, He spoke of Heaven as His Home, and of God as His Father.

He said: "I came out from the Father. I came into the world. I shall leave the world and go unto my Father."

He takes the terror out of death; He takes the fear out of life.

For there is a Heaven home.

He introduced the New Law of the New Covenant.

John 13:34-35: "A new commandment I give unto you, that ye love one another; even as I have loved you, that ye also love one another. By this shall all men know that ye are my disciples, if ye have love one to another."

This was to supersede the Old Covenant Law.

He had commanded them to love in the Old Covenant Law, but they could not do it.

Now He recreated them with His own nature which is love, so that it became natural for men to love now.

I John 4:7-8, "Beloved, let us love one another: for love is of God, and every one that loveth is begotten of God, and knoweth God. He that loveth not, knoweth not God; for God is love."

The new Greek word "Agape" that Jesus evidently coined is used here.

Everyone who has this love is begotten of God.

Isn't that a remarkable statement?

Only those who have Agapa are born of God.

I John 3:14, "We know that we have passed out of death into life because we love the brethren."

And now He says so clearly: "He that loveth not, knoweth not God, because God is love."

That is the test of the New Birth.

That is the new thing, the mightiest thing that ever came into the human life.

You see it is Eternal Life, the nature of the Father, that has made us love.

We are begotten of love.

Selfishness reigns in the human heart naturally.

Selfishness is deposed, dethroned. And a new nature, the love nature of God takes its place.

It was the Beginning of the Body of Christ.

This strong new organism is a spiritual thing.

Its Head is seated at the Right Hand of the Majesty on High.

We have become united with Him in a spirit union.

He likens it to the vine and the branch.

Paul in I Corinthians 12: likens it to the physical body.

But one truth outshines everything else in that mythical union; it is our utter oneness with Him and with one another.

We are actually one with Him.

We died with Him, were buried with Him, suffered with Him, were justified with Him, made alive with Him, conquered Satan with Him, were raised from the dead with Him, and now we are seated with Him.

We reign in life with Him.

We actually belong to royalty.

We are as much a part of Jesus as He and the Father are a part of each other.

His very substance and being is in us.

I wonder what would happen to us if we meditated about our oneness with Christ, our union with the Body of Christ.

I Cor. 12:12-30 should be read over and over again. We cannot take space to quote it.

It was the beginning of men having a hope of immortality for their bodies.

The physical body is now mortal, because of the fall.

Now every person who receives eternal life has the promise of immortality for his body when Jesus returns.

Then our bodies will never die again.

We will live in them throughout eternity.

They will be glorified bodies.

No sickness or disease can ever touch them.

I suppose that was the reason God forbade the Jews to mark or cut their bodies.

That is the reason He tells us in I Cor. 6:19 "that our bodies are holy, sacred to God, and we are to glorify God in them."

Romans 12:1-2: "I beseech you therefore, brethren, by the mercies of God, to present your bodies a living sacrifice, holy, acceptable to God, which is your spiritual service. And be not fashioned according to this world: but be ye transformed by the renewing of your mind, that ye may prove what is the good and acceptable and perfect will of God."

We are to offer up our bodies as living sacrifices.

He says that our bodies are for the Lord.

"And know ye not that your bodies are members of Christ and that your bodies are not your own."

They have been bought with a price.

What a study that would make to go through the entire Word and find out how sacred the human body is to the Father and how sacred it should be to us.

It was the beginning of the believer's victory over Satan.

Satan had been man's master through all the ages since the Fall.

He was now to taste the bitterness of being subordinated to the Man whom he had subjugated to sin.

Jesus has given man a legal right to use His Name which has all authority over Satan.

How fearless it makes one when he knows the power and the authority of the Name of Jesus.

"Whatsoever ye shall ask of the Father in my name, I will give to you."

Satan is the only hindering power to prayer.

We can brush him aside and take our rights in the matchless Name.

When a mother knows that it is an evil spirit that has come into the child which makes it disobedient, she can drive it out with that precious Name.

When any evil habit lays hold of us, that Name brings deliverance.

Man, this New Man, is God's Master Man.

The Beginning of the Love Way

Jesus introduced a new way of Life, a new way of living.

He gave us the ability to live this new way.

We were to be subordinated to the love life that belongs to the New Creation.

We are to walk in love, think love and do love.

It is going to solve the home problem.

There will be no more quarreling and breaking of fellowship.

No more wrecking the homes and lives and turning children over to be reared by other people.

It is going to be a new kind of living.

Selfishness seeks its own happiness.

That is the reason that a mother can become a cigarette fiend and blast the baby's nervous system before it is born. She can hang around the cocktail parlors and listen to vile stories and neglect her children and her home. She does not have the new kind of life.

This new thing that Jesus brought has glorified motherhood, made babies and wifehood sacred.

"It seeketh not its own "

It never goes to a divorce court.

It does not wrangle over property.

It seeks only the good of another, rather than its own.

It is the Jesus life.

It is the Jesus way in our every day walk.

It is bringing Jesus into vital contact with the world in every phase of our walk.

It is the New Law that is to govern marriage and homes.

The old Jewish law of marriage was based upon the fact that man was spiritually dead.

The new law is based upon the fact that man has been made a New Creation, created in Christ.

The Beginning of Righteousness

Among the many wonderful things that the New Creation gives us is Righteousness.

Understand, Righteousness is a new thing that Jesus brought and gave to the New Creation.

If fellowship is the climax of Redemption, then Righteousness is the means whereby fellowship can become a reality.

It means the ability to stand in the Father's presence without a sense of guilt, condemnation or inferiority.

You can stand in His presence like a son or daughter stands in the presence of a loving Father.

You have been made Righteous with His own nature.

You have become partakers of the divine nature.

You have become Righteous on legal grounds.

It is not sufferance or pity.

It is a clear-cut, legal Righteousness.

You are what He made you to be.

You have become the Righteousness of God in Christ.

It is not the result of any works that you have done.

You have simply accepted Christ as your Saviour, confessed Him as your Lord, and God made you His Righteousness in His Son.

What does that do to you?

First, it gives you a standing with the Father.

You can come boldly into the Throne Room at any time.

It makes you a master of demons and of all their works.

It makes you a conqueror over circumstances and a master of the laws of nature when it is necessary.

It makes Satan fearful of you because he recognizes that you are the Righteousness of God in Christ, and that you know you are what God says you are, and you dare to take your place and act your part.

This is a masterful thing.

Everyone of you who reads this should go to the depths of it.

Enjoy what belongs to you.

You will honor the Father by daring to act as a son should act, in the Father's presence or in any crisis that may arise.

Righteousness takes away sin consciousness, the sense of unworthiness, that old feeling of weakness and lack of ability.

You are a master under God.

If I dared, I would tell you that you have become God's superman.

There is no limit to what you can do in Christ.

You have become the fruit bearing part of Christ.

That means that the work that Jesus began to do, you can accomplish.

You are no longer slaves to men, circumstances, disease, or any kind of Satanic tyranny.

The Revelation of a Love Slave

For a long time I wondered what the Greek word "Doulos" really meant.

Romans 1:1 is a good illustration, "Paul a servant of Jesus Christ."

I notice that nowhere in the Pauline Revelation is man called a servant of God but once. And that is an interpolation.

It should be "a servant of Jesus Christ."

Let me give you a new translation that perfectly fits the thing.

"Paul, (or the little one) a love slave of Jesus Christ."

You see, Jesus was the first love slave.

His love drove Him to perform all the miracles that blessed humanity.

Love drove Him to the cross.

Love made Him a Substitute for sin.

Love keeps Him now as a Mediator and Intercessor and Saviour at the Father's right hand.

He has not had a vacation in nearly two thousand years.

He is a love slave.

When I saw that I might become a love slave, it seemed as though my heart dreams were to be realized. A love slave of Jesus !

It means living and walking under the impulses of love, not seeking my own, but His, not having my own way.

Can you imagine what it means for one to say, "I love my Master, I love my great Father God."

I choose this love slave life.

I become a slave of the Body of Christ.

I live to perfect every believer.

I live to awaken them to their rights and privileges, to unveil to them their riches in Christ, the hidden riches of grace and love.

I am not seeking my own; I found it in Christ.

Money has lost its value except to help others and glorify the Master.

Sense knowledge is as trash for the excellency of the knowledge that will make me a better love slave.

Now I can understand, "Seeketh not its own." Has no dream but others' happiness and their growth in grace.

I used to wonder about Col. 1:28: "That I may present every man perfect in Christ, whereunto I labor also, striving according to his working, which worketh in me mightily."

A love slave was speaking to me last night and she said: "I could not understand why I found myself on my knees sobbing."

It was the Spirit's intercession in you. He was crying through you over someone.

But she said, "I did not understand it."

I said, "It was not necessary. He knew what He was after and you were His yielded instrument."

I have been so overwhelmed at times that the Spirit was interceding through my Spirit.

I was a love slave. I was taking Jesus' place, weeping over the unsaved.

I was speaking in Chicago about the love slave.

A very brilliant young man came up at the close of the service and said, "Mr. Kenyon, do you suppose He would enroll me as a love slave?"

I said, "Suppose you apply. Just ask Him about it."

He became one of God's choice ones, one of His used ones.

You, who are reading this, have been mightily moved over some of these messages in my books.

But I wonder if you have been like an iceberg and melted while the sun was beating upon you and then froze up as soon as the sun went down. Stirred while you were reading or listening, but as soon as you touched the world again, other emotions were awakened and you forgot.

The Love Slave

When I would falter and stop on the way
My heart lose courage and I fail to pray,
Remind me, dear Lord, of that cross on the hill,
Of the Man who hung there, Love's mission to fill.

When I am tempted to forget my call,
Abandon my mission, forsake it all,
Remind me dear Lord, of that cross on the hill,
Of the Man who hung there, Love's mission to fill.

Stir in my being, a passion, dear Lord,
To fulfill Thy mission, herald thy Word,
'Til every nation shall hear the glad song
Of His redemption, They've waited so long.

Jesus evidently walked in the light of His confession.

He was what He confessed.

It is strange we never knew until recently that faith follows in the footprints of our confession.

Our confession builds the road over which faith hauls its mighty cargo.

You are going to learn that you never rise above your confession.

You will never enjoy the riches of grace until you confess them.

You are going to find that your confession of what He is, what He has done for you, and what you are in Him, always preceeds His revelation of Himself.

Salvation follows confession. "For if thou shalt confess with thy mouth Jesus as Lord."

And the same is true in receiving the Holy Spirit.

Our healing follows our confession.

Some people have to "hold fast to their confession" in the face of apparent defeat. They refuse to give in to sense evidences.

You are going to learn the danger of a dual confession: confessing one moment the absolute integrity of the Word, but the next moment confessing that He has not made it good in your case.

Your confession is the thing that challenges the world.

It is the thing that causes them to venture in the faith life.

Christianity is the great Confession.

It heads up in Jesus in His confession; and next in us in our bold declaration of the utter truthfulness of the living Word.

≡||≡||≡||≡||≡||≡||≡||≡||≡||≡||≡||≡||≡||≡||≡||≡||≡||≡||≡|||

Chapter XXII

OUR CONFESSION

REALIZATION can only follow confession.

We walk in the light of our testimony.

The word becomes real only as we confess its reality.

Satan fears our testimony. If you confess something with your mouth, it reacts upon your heart or your spirit.

We confess what we are in Christ, then we act our confession.

If we confess our fears, they will rule us.

If we confess the dominion of disease, it asserts its lordship over our bodies more fully.

If we confess our freedom, that the Son has made us free, God makes that confession a reality.

When we realize that Jesus met defeat and conquered it, and we dare to make that confession, defeat and failure lose their dominion over us.

Thinking faith thoughts and speaking faith words, leads the heart out of defeat into victory.

When we confess His Word, He watches over it to make it good, but there is no action on the part of God without our confession.

Christianity is called the "Great Confession."

Heb. 3:1: "Consider the Apostle and High Priest of our confession, even Jesus." (Am. Rev.)

Heb. 4:14: "Having then a great high priest, who hath passed through the heavens, Jesus the Son of God, let us hold fast our confession."

What is the confession to which we are to hold fast? That in Him we have a perfect redemption.

Col. 1:13-14: "Who delivered us out of the authority of darkness, and translated us into the kingdom of the Son of His love; in whom we have our redemption, the remission of our sins."

That Redemption never becomes a reality until we confess it; few seem to grasp this fact.

In the face of apparent defeat, we confess our Redemption and deliverance, and it becomes a reality.

We do not ask for Redemption; we thank Him for it.

That Redemption was wrought according to I Pet. 1:18-19, "Knowing that ye were redeemed, not with corruptible things, with silver or gold, from your vain manner of life handed down from your fathers; but with precious blood, as of a lamb without blemish and without spot, even the blood of Christ." This is not a promise, but a fact.

Eph. 2:10: We confess that we are New Creations, created in Christ Jesus, "For we are His workmanship, created in Christ Jesus for good works, which God afore prepared that we should walk in them."

II Cor. 5:17, We dare to say, "Old things are passed away: behold, all things are become new, all these things are of God, who reconciled us to Himself through Christ."

We know that we are not only redeemed and made New Creations, but that we are also reconciled. We dare confess it before the world.

We confess our Redemption from the hand of Satan, that he is unable to put disease upon us and hold us in bondage.

Rev. 12:11: "And they overcame him because of the blood of the lamb, and because of the word of their testimony."

The word here is "Logos." They overcame the adversary, because of the blood of the Lamb, and the logos that was in their testimony. They rested on the integrity of the Word.

They dared to confess that what God said was true.

Romans 4:25: "Who was delivered up for our trespasses, and was raised for our justification."

Rom. 5:1: "Being therefore justified by faith, we have peace with God through our Lord Jesus Christ."

Then dare confess that this is true now.

Confess your righteousness in Christ.

We are now the Righteousness of God in Christ.

We dare declare this before the world.

We dare confess that God, Himself, has become our Righteousness. Rom. 3:26.

II Cor. 5:21: We have been made by the New Birth and the Spirit, the very Righteousness of God in Him. "Him who knew no sin He made to be sin on our behalf; that we might become the Righteousness of God in Him."

This is God's own declaration of what we are now; not what we want to be, but what God has made us to be.

I Pet. 2:24 declares we are healed. "Who His own self bare our sins in His body upon the tree, that we, having died unto sins, might live unto righteousness; by whose stripes ye were healed."

The work is done.

It is not a problem of getting our healing, nor a problem of faith. It is a problem of the integrity of the Word of God.

Can we depend upon that Word?

Jer. 1:12: "I watch over my Word to perform it."

Our confession must be a confession of the absolute faithfulness of the Word, of His finished work, and of the reality of our relationship as sons and daughters.

Our words determine our faith.

Our words are our confession.

If I continually confess lack; I believe in lack; my confession surely becomes a reality.

I confess the things which I believe.

If I believe in failure and weakness, I will confess it.

I will live up to the standard of my confession.

If I dare say that Ps. 34:10 is true, "But they that seek Jehovah shall not want any good thing," and if I stand by my confession, God will make good all I have confessed

Ps. 84:11: "No good thing will He withhold from them that walk uprightly. O Jehovah of Hosts, blessed is the man that trusteth in thee."

I dare confess Pr. 3:5, "Trust in Jehovah with all thy heart, and lean not upon shine own understanding: in all thy ways acknowledge Him, and He will direct thy paths."

That is guidance.

Not only is it deliverance from conditions, but it is a guidance into His will, into the paths of plenty.

Phil. 4:19 becomes the song of my heart, "And my God shall supply every need of yours according to His riches in glory in Christ Jesus."

What a confession this is. The heart waxes strong.

Is. 54:17: "No weapon that is formed against thee shall prosper; and every tongue that shall rise against thee in judgment thou shalt condemn. This is the heritage of the servants of Jehovah, and their righteousness which is of me saith Jehovah."

God is under obligation to stand by and care for His own. He cannot fail us.

Ps. 118:6: "Jehovah is on my side; I will not fear: What can man do unto me?"

Is. 41:10: "Fear thou not, for I am with thee; be not dismayed for I am thy God: I will strengthen thee; yea, I will help thee; yea, I will uphold thee with the right hand of my righteousness."

This is God's challenge, and I dare confess it before the world. What a confession it makes!

God says to me personally: "Don't be afraid, child, I am with thee. Be not dismayed; I am your God."

He was Israel's God. Do you remember what happened to Pharoah and Egypt, and the Philistines? Ex. 14:21-31, I Sam. 14:

Do you remember what happened to all the nations that laid their hands upon Israel, while they were keeping the Covenant?

I Chron. 16:22: "Touch not mine anointed ones."

He will take care of us as He took care of them. He will be our Protector and Caretaker.

Jesus said that faith would win. Faith has won. We are witnesses of this tremendous reality.

The Bible is God's confession. The more I read it, the more this great truth overshadows everything from Genesis to Revelation.

159

It is a continual confession of His greatness, His ability, His love, and His great Father heart.

Jesus, as you see Him in the four Gospels, is continually making confessions.

He is the Great Shepherd; He is the Light of the World.

John 10:11: "I am the good shepherd; the good shepherd layeth down his life for the sheep."

John 8:12: "I am the light of the world; he that followeth me shall not walk in the darkness, but shall have the light of life."

He said (Jn. 14:6): "I am the way, and the truth and the life."

John 11:25: "I am the Resurrection and the life."

John 6:35: "I am the bread of life."

Those are tremendous confessions.

Jn. 10:29: "My Father, who hath given them unto me, is greater than all; and no one is able to snatch them out of the Father's hand."

Jesus' confession led Him straight to Calvary.

Jn. 5:18: "For this cause therefore the Jews sought the more to kill Him, because He not only breaks the sabbath, but also called God his own Father, making Himself equal with God."

The fearless confessions of men down through the ages have given to us our martyrs.

Faith gives courage to confession, and confession gives boldness to faith.

Your confession lines you up, gives you your place, establishes your position.

We know what you are. If you are silent, we cannot place you.

Confession heals, or confession keeps you sick.

By your confession, you are saved or lost.

By your confession, you have plenty, or you lack.

By your confession, you are weak, or you are strong.

You are what you confess with your lips, and what you believe in your heart.

Your confession of failure keeps you in the realm of failure.

Your confession of God's ability in your case, puts you over.

Pr. 6:2: "Thou art snared with the words of thy mouth, Thou art taken with the words of thy mouth."

We are snared by our confession, or we are set free with the words of our confession.

Make your confession harmonize with the Word of God.

It will not harmonize with Sense Knowledge. Don't try to make it.

Sense knowledge calls it presumption or fanaticism, but God calls it faith and honors it.

Heb. 11:1: "Now faith is assurance of things hoped for, a conviction of things not seen."

God has done all that can be done for us.

He says that His Redemption is complete.

You confess that it is done, taking your place, calling yourself by the name that He has called you, acknowledging all the Word says is yours.

You now declare that all God has spoken, in your case is true.

Jn. 8:32,36: "And ye shall know the truth, and the truth shall make you free."

"If therefore the Son shall make you free, ye shall be free indeed."

The truth will make you free. You declare that whom the Son has made free is free in reality, that sin cannot lord it over you any longer, that disease and sickness cannot lord it over you.

Romans 6:14: "For sin shall not have dominion over you," or "lord it over you."

Worry and anxiety cannot lord it over you. Satan's dominion is ended.

You stand complete in Him.

Few of us have realized the power of His Word on our lips.

He said in Mark 16:18 that those who believe "shall lay hands on the sick and they shall recover."

John 14:13: "Whatsoever ye shall ask (demand) in my Name, that will I do."

Acts 3: deals with the story of the Name in Peter's lips. He said, "look on us.... In the name of Jesus Christ of Nazareth, walk."

If you do not use the Name, the Name can do nothing.

But if you will use the Name, it will be as the Father's Name was in Jesus' lips.

In Acts 4:18-37 we are reminded of how the place was shaken by the name of Jesus.

18th verse, "and they called them, and charged them not to speak at all nor teach in the name of Jesus."

The Name in their lips had shaken Jerusalem to the foundation.

Acts 16:16-8 shows the power of the Name in Paul's lips.

He said, "I charge thee in the name of Jesus Christ to come out of her." She was healed and delivered.

John 15:7: "If ye abide in me, and my words abide in you, ask whatsoever ye will, and it shall be done unto you."

The Word in your lips not only makes you free, but it sets others free.

The Word in your lips heals the sick.

The Word in your lips creates faith in the hearts of those who hear you.

The Word in your lips will change lives as they listen.

It is the very life of God in those words.

The Bible is God's Word.

In the lips of love and faith every Word is God-filled.

Our daily conversation is the Great Confession.

We confess Christ before the world.

We confess the fulness of His grace.

We confess the integrity of the Revelation.

Our first confession is Romans 10:9-10: "Because if thou shalt confess with thy mouth Jesus as Lord, and shalt believe in thy heart that God raised Him from the dead, thou shalt be saved: for with the heart man believeth unto righteousness; and with the mouth confession is made unto salvation."

We have found a perfect Redemption. We confess it to the world.

In Acts 10:36 Peter says, "He is Lord of All." How that thrills the Heart.

He is the Lord of the three worlds: heaven, earth, and hell.

Every knee bows to that Name.

With joy we confess Ps. 23:1, "The Lord is my shepherd; I shall not want."

Jer. 16:19: "O Jehovah, my strength, and my stronghold, and my refuge in the day of affliction."

Phil. 4:13: "I can do all things in Christ who strengtheneth me."

I say to the world: "The Lord Jesus is my supply. He is my shepherd; I do not want."

There is a grave danger of our making a wrong confession, a wrong affirmation.

We confess our fears and doubts. That gives Satan dominion.

We confess our sickness and that confession binds our will as a captive and holds us in absolute slavery.

We confess want and lack of money, and want comes like an armed man and holds us in bondage.

We confess lack of ability, in the face of the fact that God said He was the strength of our life.

These confessions of failure shut the Father out, and let Satan in; give him the right-of-way.

These confessions repudiate the Word of God. They honor Satan.

What should we confess?

Ps. 23:1: "The Lord is my shepherd; I do not want."

You are not afraid anymore, and you confess it.

Jn. 10:29: "My Father is greater than all."

Our words imprison us, or they set us free. Our words put us in bondage, keep us from our freedom and our liberty in Christ.

Mal. 3:13: "Your words have been stout against me, saith Jehovah."

That is when our words war with His Word.

A woman came to me the other day. She said, "Mr. Kenyon, I have been prayed for, but I get no deliverance." Her word contradicted the Word of God.

His Word said, "If ye shall ask anything of the Father, He will give it you in my Name."

Mk. 16:18: "They that believe . . . shall lay hands on the sick and they shall recover."

She repudiated it; she denied that the Word was true. Her words were warring against the Word of God.

She had unconsciously taken an attitude of mind that was against the Word.

She did not intend to, but she had done it.

That very attitude held her in bondage.

As I talked with her, I could see that she was not taking in what I said.

When I prayed for her, she was freed from pain, but the whine did not leave her voice. There was no confession of victory in her lips.

There is always a danger of a Mental Assent confession.

Mental Assent recognizes the truthfulness of the Word, but never acts upon it.

Its confession is: "Oh yes, there is healing in the Word. There is salvation and deliverance in the Word, but . . ."

On the other hand, faith joyfully confesses its victory. Its joy is a celebration; it is a triumph over the witnesses of the Senses.

Faith gives a sense of security, of absolute assurance, of quietness and when this breaks forth in confession, it becomes a reality.

The heart must be rooted and grounded in the Word, and in love.

Acts 19:20, "So mightily grew the Word of the Lord and prevailed."

Faith is simply the Word prevailing over sense evidence.

Acts 20:32 gives us a striking illustration. "And now I commend you to God, and to the Word of His grace, which is able to build you up, and to give you the inheritance among all them that are sanctified."

It is the Word that establishes; it is the Word that builds.

It is the Word of His grace that builds faith into the heart of the believer.

Jesus' confession demands more careful attention.

Jn. 5:19-20: Here are ten claims of Jesus. Everyone of them puts Him into the class of Deity. Read them carefully. Underscore them in your Bible.

Jn. 5:43: "I came in my Father's Name."

Jn. 5:46: "For if ye believed Moses, ye would believe me."

Jn. 6:35: "I am the bread of life: he that cometh to me shall not hunger, and he that believeth on me shall never thirst."

This is a tremendous confession.

Jn. 6:47: "He that believeth hath Eternal Life. . . . I am the living bread which came down out of heaven."

Jn. 7:29: "I know Him; because I am from Him, and He sent me."

Jn. 8:29: "I do always the things that are pleasing to Him."

Jn. 10:10: "I came that they may have Life, and may have it abundantly."

Jn 10.30: "I and the Father are one."

Jn 11:25: "I am the resurrection, and the life: he that believeth on me, though he die, yet shall ye live."

These are a few of His confessions. Do we dare to confess what we are in Christ and what we have in Christ?

Dare we confess Jn. 1:16? "Of His fulness have we all received, and grace upon grace."

We have received His fulness, but it has done us no good for we have failed to translate it into a confession.

Every believer knows that God laid his diseases on Jesus; yet he fears to make the confession and act on the Word.

This fear is of the Adversary. It indicates that we have more confidence in the Adversary than we have in the Word of God.

We confess that what He says is true.

Then we demonstrate it in our daily life.

There is no confession in the lives of many people.

There is much prayer, but there is no confession that the Word is true. It is not prayer many need, but confession of the Word.

I do not mean a confession of sin.

A woman said recently after I had prayed for her and opened the Word to her, "You will keep on praying for my disease, won't you?"

Her confession was that the Word was a lie.

You are to confess, that you can do what He says you can do, that you are what the Word says you are.

He says that you are a New Creation created in Christ Jesus.

He says that you are more than a victor; that you are an overcomer.

He made you to be a son, a daughter of God Almighty, an heir of God and a joint heir of Jesus Christ.

You can do all things in Him who is your strength. Phil. 4:13.

What He says I can do, I declare that I can do.

What He says I am, I declare that I am.

I make my confession boldly.

You make your confession: "God is my Father; I am His child. As a son in His family, I am taking my place. I am acting my part. I am in Christ. Christ is in me."

You remember that the Father will be to you what you confess Him to be.

If prayer is not answered, hold fast to your confession.

If the Name of Jesus does not give instant deliverance; hold fast your confession.

If the money does not come, stand by your confession.

Lu. 1:37: "No Word from God is void of power."

Is. 55:11: The Word must accomplish the will of the Father.

"So shall my word be that goeth forth out of my mouth: it shall not return unto me void, but it shall accomplish that which I please, and it shall prosper in the thing whereto I sent it."

There is a danger of praying, then going back on your prayer.

When you pray for some need, and declare that the need is not met, you have repudiated your prayer.

But prayer is answered.

His Word is real.

Do not annul the Word by a negative confession.

Is. 41:10: "Fear thou not, for I am with thee; be not dismayed, for I am thy God; I will strengthen thee; yea, I will help thee; yea, I will uphold thee with the right hand of my Righteousness."

Claiming Your Own

Hebrews 11:1: "Now faith is giving substance to things hoped for; the evidence of things not seen."

Another translation, "Faith is the title deed to things prayed for; the evidence that they are yours before they are seen."

Faith is counting prayer answered before the Father has acted.

Jesus said, "All things whatsoever you pray and ask for, believe that ye have received them and ye shall have them." R.V.

This is not a promise.

This is a statement of fact.

This is the title deed to the things prayed for.

Faith is our bill of rights.

You see, that when you are born again, you enter into the New Covenant; you become a part of that New Covenant.

You become a member of it, and all that was purchased in that redemption is yours, and all that you were redeemed from, you are free from; His redemption sets you free from the dominion of sin, the authority of sin, the guilt of sin, and the uncleanness of sin.

You are free from that.

You are free from everything.

That redemption freed you.

You are not only free, but you own all His redemption purchased for you. You have a right to everything that redemption carried, but when will you understand it?

We are free, redeemed, and yet we sit around on the curb stone in front of our mansion that we have inherited and cry for faith and wisdom to enter in through the door that is open.

Without knowing it, our ministry has paralyzed us so that we are unable to arise and take what belongs to us, and yet in Colossians the first chapter and twelfth verse Rotherham makes it read "Thanks be unto God who has made us sufficient for our share of the inheritance of the saints in life."

He has made us sufficient to enjoy all our riches, to enjoy our perfect deliverance, and made us sufficient to walk in the fullness of our redemption in Christ.

There is no ground for our being weak; no reason for our being failures.

We have no right to be conquered and dishonored.

The whole plan and scheme of the Father heart of God is that we should walk in the fulness of the Divine Life.

When He says, "Ye are complete in Him," He means it.

That is, the fulness of this life.

That is, our chartered rights.

Satan absolutely has no dominion over us.

We have been translated out of the authority of darkness, and we have been translated into the Kingdom of the Son of His love, in whom we have our complete redemption now.

But how it dishonors Him for us to be weak and floundering and hesitant.

How it dishonors Him for us to talk of doubts and to pray for faith in Him.

We have no more business to deal in doubts than we have to deal in contraband goods.

We have no more right to deal in doubts than we have in narcotics.

Doubts are of the devil, and to honor doubts is to honor Satan; to honor unbelief is to dishonor God.

We are to think in terms of faith, to use the language of faith, to walk in the realm of faith, and to refuse any other walk.

We are the sons of God and are to walk as the first Son did when He walked on earth.

We bear about in our bodies the resurrection power of Jesus; the life of Jesus.

We have in our bodies the great mighty Holy Spirit.

He makes our bodies His temples.

We have all the power there is.

We have it now.

Have you Jesus?

You say, "Yes."

Well, if you have Jesus, you have everything.

Use your rights.

Use your privileges.

Let Jesus Christ be big in you.
Count on Him rather than weakness.
Count on Him rather than circumstances.
Count on Him rather than the arm of flesh.
Rest in Him.
Take your place in Him
Give Him his place in your life.

Do it now, and say to your heart, "I am more than a conqueror: I am more than a victor; I am identified with the very Son of God; He is identified with me. Now live and let Him live in you.

This is one of the greatest dramas of Divine Grace.

We are to accept the challenge of Love, and use our Father's ability in our daily walk.

This chapter is a challenge to the reader.

This is where you are to count up your riches in Christ. You will add them with God's own divine method of adding and your heart will whisper, "this is what I have been after."

"This is what I have been longing for, but did not know how to receive it."

You can enter the philosopher's dream land.

You can live from now on in the wonder land of the supernatural, with Him.

You will know the reality of the branch and vine life.

You will experience the relationship of a son to the Father God.

You will know that wisdom and ability belong to you in Christ.

You are in the realm of life in its fulness.

Chapter XXIII

OUR RESPONSE TO GOD'S ABILITY

S the modern church at her best; a true representative of the church of which Paul spoke in his Epistles? Are we walking in the fulness of our privilege? Is the world receiving from us the benefits of the Divine Life that should be theirs?

This is a study in "What we possess in Christ." It is what really belongs to us, in this Divine Life.

There is no doubt but what God planned that the church should be composed of supermen and women.

Men and women who conquered sickness and disease, who ruled circumstances, who turned weakness into strength, failure into success and took the weak things of this world and confounded the mighty.

Let us look at our inheritance in Christ. Jn. 1:16: "Of His fulness have we all received and grace upon grace."

What is His fulness? It is completeness. In Him is everything that humanity needs. He represents all of the Father's heart desires for humanity.

He is the bank upon which the heart of man can draw to completion. "Of His fulness have we all received."

We have not received part.

But everyone of us have received His fulness.

There is fulness of love so that we shall rise above selfishness and "seek not our own." There is such a complete fulness of love that we cannot fail, because love never fails.

There is the love that led Jesus to save us. It is love that gains the mastery until we cry with Paul II Cor. 5:14-15: "For the love of Christ constraineth us; because we thus judge, that one died for all, therefore all died; and He died for all, that they that live, should no longer live unto themselves, but unto Him, who for their sakes died and rose again."

There is not only His fulness of love, but there is a fulness of freedom in the Redemptive work of Christ so that no believer need live with the sense of bondage and limitation, as he lives in the fulness of Christ's liberty, the fulness of His complete and perfect Redemption.

Eph. 1:7: "In whom we have our Redemption through His blood, the remission of our trespasses, according to the riches of His grace."

No one can measure the limitlessness of that Redemption. Redemption is ours, not as a theory or as a great doctrine, about which to argue, but as a living, sweet, beautiful reality for our daily lives.

"Of His fulness" of rest, quietness, of assurance have we received. This is the mother of faith.

This is where the Divine Life leads into the very heart of the Son of God and rests in His quietness.

Follow the Master from the time of His arrest until He died on the cross. There is no excitement, no restlessness, no impatience.

He is the absolute master of the circumstances surrounding the crucifixion.

Of His quietness have we all received. Is. 32:17: "And the work of Righteousness shall be peace; and the effect of Righteousness, quietness and confidence forever."

There is an abundance, an utter fulness of this quietness that grows out of Righteousness.

He has become our Righteousness; and He, out of His Righteousness, His quietness, His supremacy over everything that is antagonistic to our hearts, has brought us quietness.

We rest in His rest. Ps. 37:3-7 gives us a picture of restfulness and quietness. "Trust in Jehovah, and do good: Dwell in the land, and feed on His faithfulness." The heart is no longer feeding upon failure and weakness, but it is delighting itself in Jehovah and finding the desires of its heart. Everything has been committed to Him; everything is trusted into His hands.

Now out of that trust there flows the quiet rest.

There is no more fretting or irritation.

We are resting.

His fulness is our fulness.

Jesus' completeness is our completeness.

Eph. 1:22-23: "And He put all things in subjection under His feet, and gave Him to be head over all things to the church, which is His body, the fulness of Him that filleth all in all."

Every power has been put under His feet.

We are His body.

We are His feet.

Satan's dominion has been broken.

We are put into the place of mastery.

It is not the result of our struggling and praying.

We inherited it.

His completeness is the fulness of victory.

All things are under His feet.

He gave Christ to be head over all things. We are seated with Him in the heavenlies. Eph. 2:6: "He raised us up with Him and made us to sit with Him in the heavenlies, in Christ Jesus.

We are seated there now in the mind of the Father. All authority, dominion, disease, sickness, and failure are beneath our feet.

Eph. 3:16-20: "That He would grant you, according to the riches of His glory, that ye may be strengthened with power through His Spirit in the inward man; that Christ may dwell in your hearts through faith; to the end that ye, being rooted and grounded in love, may be strong to apprehend with all the saints what is the breadth and length and height and depth, and to know the love of Christ which passeth knowledge."

That is according to His fulness. You are not to be blessed according to your conception, but according to His riches in glory.

You are to be strengthened with His strength in the inward man, that Christ may actually gain the mastery, to the end that you may be rooted and grounded in love.

To be rooted and grounded in love is the consummation of life. What more could you ask for? You will be bearing the fruit of love.

You will have the fragrance of love.

You will have the ability and power of love.

You can see that God, being love, means you will be rooted and grounded in Him, when you are rooted and grounded in love.

Out from His very heart comes pouring into you and through you the very graciousness, beauty, and riches of the Father's heart.

"That ye may be strong to grasp with all the saints what is the breadth, length, height, and depth, and to know the love of Christ which passeth knowledge."

The mind can go no farther than this. Grace reaches down and takes us by the hand and lifts us up into the Spirit realm of His fulness.

We are unconscious of ourselves, filled unto all the fulness of God. His very nature is love. We have partaken of that nature.

"Now unto Him that is able to do exceeding abundantly above all that we ask or think, according to the power that worketh in us." You talk about being weak, about being powerless in the face of such a scripture!

Put that modern testimony of uselessness over against this revelation of His fulness.

"Of His fulness have we all received." The very gates of heaven are open. He is pouring out such a blessing that our hearts cannot receive it, so He has to enlarge our hearts just as the man mentioned in Luke enlarged his barns so he would have a place to store his grains.

God has to enlarge our hearts so that we can receive of His fulness and not burst.

Eph. 4:12-13: "For the perfecting of the saints, unto the work of ministering, unto the building up of the body of Christ: till we all attain unto unity of the faith, and of the knowledge of the Son of God, unto a fullgrown man, unto the measure of the stature of the fulness of Christ."

He is aiming at perfection in us.

It is all His work.

It is the Spirit working through His Word.

What do we do?

We yield to this perfection.

We yield to this fulness.

We yield to the stream of health that flows from the stripes with healing and grace and strength, until we attain the fulness of faith and fulness of knowledge, until the very fulness of Jesus Himself controls us.

There is no place for weakness nor failure there.

Phil. 4:13: "I can do all things in Him who strengtheneth me."

We are no longer limited believers.

We are no longer living in the sense of bondage and weakness.

We are breathing in His very fulness.

No, that is not right. We are breathing out His fulness, for His fulness is in us.

Gal. 2:20, Paul said, "It is no longer I that live, but Christ liveth in me." The unfettered, the unhampered Christ is living His big life in us.

Col. 1:19, "For it was the good pleasure of the Father that in Him should all the fulness dwell."

He is not just a shaft of light from the Throne, He is the Light.

It was the good pleasure of the Father that everyone of us should partake of this fulness.

Col. 1:29, He wants to present every man perfect in Christ.

"Whereunto I labor also, striving according to his working, which worketh in me mightily."

Paul recognized that it was God who was at work within him.

Phil 2:13, "For it is God who is at work within me, willing and working his own good pleasure."

That was a thrilling, beautiful reality.

Your heart now reaches out and grasps it in all its sweet simplicity.

Col. 2:9-10 is his final challenge on the word, "Fullness." "For in him dwelleth all the fulness of the Godhead bodily and in him ye are made full, who is the head of all principality and power."

He does not try to make you full.

He simply made you full.

You rest on that; it is true.

You are what He says you are.

The problem is: are we going to use this ability that is ours?

Here is God's fulness at our disposal.

It is the most thrilling fact this side of heaven. We are united with God in Christ. It is a union of life in life.

He poured His life into us, and that life has recreated us so that now we are what He calls us in Eph. 2:10. "We are His workmanship created in Christ Jesus."

172

We are created for good works, "which He afore prepared that we should walk in them."

What are His good works?

To open the Word; to lead the weak and fearful into their inheritance.

He has prepared that good work for us.

Mark 16:17, You will find that wherever the believers went, God went with them "confirming the word with the signs that followed."

Matthew 28:18-20, "All authority has been given unto me in heaven and on earth."

> To you, I give the right,
> To use my Name and might,
> In this long and bitter fight,
> 'Till I come.

He said, "Lo, I am with you always." He is there to bless you, strengthen, to empower, to give wisdom until our whole being swings in rhythm with His will. He has not left us without authority.

Luke 24:49, "Tarry ye in the city, until ye be clothed with power from on high." The word "Power" here means ability. They did tarry and that ability came.

Then they went out and used that ability for the glory of God and the joy of men.

He is not asking us to tarry any more.

The day of tarrying is ended.

Working days are here upon us.

Our call is to go empowered with His power, filled with Himself, our lips with His words upon them.

Just as Jesus had the Father's words in His lips and they healed the sick and raised the dead, so He says for us to go out with His words on our lips now and He will "work with us and confirm the Word with the closely following signs."

John 5:24 said, "He that heareth my Word, and believeth Him that sent me, hath eternal life."

We have eternal life. John 6:47, "He that believeth on me has eternal life." Eternal life is the nature of God, that nature is ours. That nature must not be hindered in us, so that it will produce the same results in us that it wrought in Christ in His earth walk.

"Beloved now are we the Sons of God." The same mighty Spirit that wrought in Christ, is in you. You are a son now, a daughter.

Romans 8:14-16 is absolutely true and real in your life.

You are the sons and daughters of God by an actual birth of which Jesus spoke in Jn. 3:3-8. "Marvel not that I say unto thee, ye must be born from above."

You have been born of the same Spirit that conceived Jesus.

You are empowered with the same Spirit that wrought in Christ and finally raised Him from the dead.

Rom. 8:11, "But if the spirit of Him that raised up Christ from the dead will dwell in you, He that raised up Christ from the dead shall give life also to your mortal bodies by His Spirit that dwelleth in you."

That same mighty Spirit is resident in you now. Perhaps you have never given credit to the Word.

You have never read it except through doctrinal eyes.

What your creed and your doctrines taught, has governed you rather than the Word of God.

The challenge is coming for you to be bigger than your doctrines and to use the ability of God now and allow God's ability to use you.

His life and your life are blended into one.

You have received His nature.

Let that nature dominate you now.

Remember one fact, that "as He is, so are you in this world."

1 Jn. 4:17 He is the lover; you are a lover. He is the strong one. You are strong with His strength. He is the conquering one; you are too.

I Jn. 5:5: "And who is He that overcometh the world, but he that believeth that Jesus is the Son of God?"

You are born of God.

You are an overcomer.

You are a victor.

You are going to use the ability of God to bless humanity.

You are not going to talk about your sickness anymore.

Ps. 27:1 "Jehovah is my light and my salvation; Whom shall I fear? Jehovah is the strength of my life; Of whom shall I be afraid?"

He is your light. He throws light upon your pathway. "Thy Word is a lamp unto your feet, and a light unto your pathway." (Ps. 119:105) He is your salvation. That is deliverance. That is Redemption. You are Redeemed. That Redemption is not a theory nor a doctrine, nor an article of your creed.

It is one of the facts of the Word of God. You are Redeemed. God is the strength of your life.

You do not need physical strength.

You do not need man's strength.

You have God's strength.

You do not need man's fulness or wisdom or knowledge.

You have God's knowledge.

You do not need man's ability.

You have God's ability.

This lifts us into the realm of the supernatural, puts us by the side of the Man of Galilee where we belong.

Matt. 28:18 "For all authority has been given unto me, in heaven and on earth."

He sends us out with authority and ability to put things over, and accomplish things for our good and the good of humanity.

Let us recapitulate. Let us look at this superman who is in Christ, the man who has taken Jesus' place and is acting in His stead.

This superman has God's life, and has the Name of Jesus.

Phil. 2:9 "Wherefore God highly exalted Him, and gave unto Him the Name which is above every name; that in the Name of Jesus every knee should bow, of beings in heaven and beings on earth, and beings under the earth and that every tongue should confess that Jesus Christ is Lord, to the glory of God the Father."

That Name restores to man the lost authority of Adam.

Every child of God has a legal right to its use.

That is God's ability.

Every child of God can have God in him if he wishes.

All you have to do is to follow Lu. 11:13. "How much more shall your heavenly Father give the Holy Spirit to them that ask Him?"

You ask Him for the Holy Spirit. He cannot do much in us until He lives in us.

Phil. 2:13 "For it is God who is at work within you, willing and working His own good pleasure."

1 Jn. 4:4 "Ye are of God, my little children, and have overcome them: because greater is He that is in you than he that is in the world."

That puts you on top of things.

That makes you a master, an overcomer in this old battle of life.

You not only have God in you, but Rom. 8:31 declares that God is for you. "If God is for us, who is against us." You have God for you. He is on your side. You are not alone.

What He said to Jehosophat in II Chron. 20:16-17, He says to you.

You not only have God with you, and God for you, but you are among the very sons of God. You have a right to go in and out of the presence of your Father God.

You are by nature heirs of God and joint heirs with Christ. You are not servants.

You are not hired men.

You are the sons of God, beloved in Jesus.

You have a legal right in the prayer life.

To you, prayer is no longer based upon sufferance nor pity, but it is based upon the Word of God.

You are legally sons.

You are legally ambassadors.

You have been given a legal right to the use of Jesus' Name in your prayer life.

Jn. 15:7 "If ye abide in me, and my words abide in you, ask

whatsoever ye will, and it shall be done unto you."

Jn. 16:24 "Hitherto have ye asked nothing in my name: ask, and ye shall receive, that your joy may be made full."

He has given you the power of attorney to use His Name. That Name is above every name.

You swing free and take your rights in Christ and make the devil afraid of God's words in your lips. Disease cannot stand in the presence of that Name on your lips.

Heaven honors that Name on our lips. Heaven is back of it.

Disease and sickness yield their right to it. The laws of nature yield to it on our lips. Circumstances become its servants, demons obey it.

Go use that mighty Name.

Remember I John 4:4, "Ye are of God." Just as Lord Nelson said to his army, "You are of England." So the Word is saying to you to-day, "Ye are of God."

The "In Christ" fact is the vital side of the Plan of Redemption; it is always in the present tense."

Wherefore if any man is in Christ, he is a New Creation."

The New Birth is an "In Him" fact.

Righteousness comes to us, "In Him."

"There is therefore now no condemnation to them that are in Christ."

When we were born again, we came into Christ.

That is the vine and the branch life.

You are grafted into Christ.

You become a part of Christ.

His nature flows through you.

His ability belongs to you.

Just as your blood flows through your body, so does eternal life flow through you.

We cannot understand it any more than we can understand the circulation of blood in our own body.

It is "In whom we have our Redemption."

Satan's dominion, power and authority are broken over you, "In Him."

"We are blessed with every spiritual blessing in Him."

We have come into the New Life of oneness "In Him."

"In Him was life and that life was the light of men."

I am "In Him."

In Him are hidden all the treasures of wisdom and life, and I am "In Him."

Chapter XXIV

SOME "IN HIM" FACTS

IT is very important that the believer know the difference between the legal side of redemption and the vital.

The legal is always in the past tense.

It is what God has done for us in Christ.

The legal begins on the cross and ends when Christ sat down at the Right Hand of the Father.

The vital begins with the New Birth and ends when we leave our personal habitation, the body, and go to be with the Lord.

The vital is what He is doing in me today, taking the things of Christ and building them into me.

It began when I first accepted Christ as my Saviour and confessed Him as my Lord.

The Holy Spirit overshadowed me and poured into my spirit eternal life, the nature of the Father, and I became His child.

All that He did for me can be done in me; His word becomes a part of me.

He opens it up to me.

He unveils Himself in it.

He begins to build the Word into my spirit as I practice it, as I come to understand its spiritual significance, and I become Jesus like.

John 15:7 is a good illustration. "If ye abide in me and my words abide in you, ye shall ask what ye will, and it shall be done unto you. Herein is my Father glorified, that ye bear much fruit; so shall ye be my disciples."

Now notice what that means.

"If ye abide in me." When I was born again, I came into Christ.

That is the vital aspect of divine life.

This illustrates it. "I am the vine and ye are the branches."

The branch is in the vine. It is part of the vine.

We are a part of the vine.

Now, "If my word abides in you."

The Word lives in me in the measure that I practice it.

My spirit feeds on the Word just as my body feeds on food.

So, as I meditate on the Word, I let it have free course in me, teaching and governing me. Then I recognize its lordship over me as I would recognize the lordship of the Master if He were here in the room.

That Word is a part of the Father Himself, and the Father is love.

So I let the Word live through me while the Spirit builds the love nature of the Father into me.

Then He says, "Ye shall ask what ye will."

One translator says, "demand your rights."

That means taking my place as a son.

I am a member of the family.

I have come to appreciate my position in Christ, and I am laboring together with Him.

I am taking Jesus' place in His absence.

I am doing the Father's will as Jesus did in His earth walk.

I am not a slave; I am a son.

I am a love son, and I am carrying out the will of my Father.

And so, now having the Word built into me, I have come to know His will.

I am not worrying about His will. I know it.

The end of that verse is very striking. "It shall be done unto you." Or, "it shall be gendered unto you," as one translator gives it.

The idea is to give birth.

It is to be borne unto you.

As Miss Rabe translates it, "If ye abide in me and my words have their place in you, you will pray to the Father, and He will create, or give birth to the thing, make it come to pass."

Because you are a branch of the vine and you are bearing God's fruit.

You are giving birth to actions that are inspired of God the Father, love actions, while He is building Himself into you.

In that next verse He says, "Herein is my Father glorified, that ye bear much love fruit."

It is a wonderful thing to bear His fruit.

John 6:63: "The words that I have spoken unto you are spirit, and are life."

They are born of the spirit and they possess the life of God.

In lips of men they recreate men.

They give courage to the faint.

They give faith to the doubter.

They transform the weak into strong.

They have in them the element that puts men over after they have been long defeated.

Let us take a very familiar passage, Col. 1:12-14, and note this translation, "Giving thanks unto the father who has given us the ability to enjoy our share of the inheritance of the saints in light."

You see He has built into me His own ability, and now His ability in me enables me to partake of my share of the thing that Christ wrought in His Substitution.

It is my inheritance.

It may be wisdom, so I will know how to use the knowledge I have gained through the Word.

It may be forbearance so that I can have joy in a hard place where everything is disagreeable, and where bitterness and selfishness run riot around me.

Or it may be forbearance, so I will be like the Master with those that are weak and selfish.

Or it may be that I need strength in my inward man, to keep me steadily in my place in life, so that I may live as the Master would live in my place.

You see, I am going to have my share of the inheritance of the saints in life.

Regardless of how much that may mean, it belongs to me.

And perhaps I will need it if I understand the next verse: "Who delivered us out of the authority of darkness, and translated us into the kingdom of the Son of his love."

So few know that they are delivered out of the authority of Satan.

They do not know that Satan has been defeated and that they were redeemed.

Satan has no legal authority over them, and they have a legal right to their liberty in Christ.

They do not know that Satan has no dominion over them now, without their personal consent to it.

They have been translated into the kingdom of the Son of His love.

Jesus said, "I am the light of the world. He that followeth me shall not walk in the darkness, but shall have the light of life."

This is a strange expression, "Light of life." But the word, life is "Zoe" which means God's life. "And God is light and in Him is no darkness at all."

You have been translated into the life realm. You are in God's realm.

You are in the beloved.

You are in Him.

You are in the family of God.

As a member of that family, you have authority over the circumstances that surround you.

Paul says in Phil. 4:11, "Not that I speak in respect of want: for I have learned, in whatsoever state I am, therein to be independent of circumstances. I know how to have sufficience and not lose my head. I know how to be abased and not lose my poise." (20th Cent. Trans.)

I have come to recognize that my Father is greater than all and that every need of mine is met.

He is the God of all ability, and He is my Father.

Now Philippians 4:13 becomes part of my daily life. "I can do all things in Him who strengtheneth me."

That is simple.

I am moving out of the realm of human weakness into the great big, wide open realm of life.

Now the fourteenth verse is suggestive. "In whom I have my redemption and the remission of my trespasses."

You see, I have my Redemption.

Satan has no dominion over me.

I have it; I am free.

I am as free as Israel was from Egypt's bondage when the Red Sea rolled upon their former masters.

The Resurrection of Jesus Christ has delivered me from my former master and set me free.

I am united, tied up, one with my seated Lord.

You see, it is no longer a life of struggling and trying.

I am in it, because He put me in it.

He took me out of bondage.

He put me in the realm of freedom.

I reign as a king through Jesus Christ, my Lord.

I pay no attention to the things that formerly filled me with fear. I am occupied with my Lord.

The Lord is my care-taker and my bread-provider and the strength of my life. Of whom, or of what, should I be afraid?

I am not afraid of disease, sickness or of old age.

The human spirit that has received the nature and the life of God knows no age.

There are no days and years to the human spirit. Days and years belong to the mortality, the body.

We have received Eternal Life into our spirits, and now we are walking in the fullness of that life.

"We walk in the light as He is in the light, and we have fellowship one with another" and with the Light-Giver.

We are not walking in darkness.

We know where we are going because He has become the light of our life.

You see there is such a reality in this union with Christ that it changes our whole outlook.

We become Righteousness conscious.

We have become the Righteousness of God in Him.

That is the end of condemnation.

That is the beginning of real fellowship.

That is the beginning of an unveiling of our rights and privileges as Sons of God.

That is the beginning of bearing fruits of Righteousness.

What a wonderful life this is.

Jesus was the first to bear the fruits of Righteousness.

Then when we were grafted into the vine, the branches became the Righteousness fruit-bearers.

We are the masters of our old slave-driver, Satan.

We are not afraid of anything the he can do because our Father is greater than all.

And Jesus said, "If a man love me, he will keep my words and my Father will love him and we will come and make our home with him.

I am not afraid of poverty or of lack of any kind, because He lives with me here.

He knows what I have in my pocketbook, and He knows what my needs are.

He knows what the bills are.

The Father himself loves me. This is beautiful.

Now I appreciate what it means to have been made Righteous with His Righteousness.

So without condemnation I walk into His presence at any time.

I never think about faith any more than a child who is walking happily and sweetly with his parents.

All that a father has belongs to his child.

All that Jesus did and is, belongs to you and me.

You see, Righteousness gives us our standing before the Father.

It is what we really are in Christ, not what He is trying to make us or what we are trying to make ourselves, but what we are by the New Creation.

Some of us are coming to be God-inside minded.

That was one of the greatest days of my life when I became conscious of the One inside.

I had asked Him to come in years before, and I knew He was there.

But I did not know how to make use of Him.

Then I remembered the Master was made unto me Righteousness and Wisdom and Sanctification and Redemption. Yet they did not mean anything to me.

I could not use the Wisdom, could not take advantage of my Righteousness, nor enjoy my Redemption.

Then the curtain was lifted. I saw the thing as it was.

The light shone in.

I was in Christ. All that He is belongs to me.

The great mighty Spirit, who raised Jesus from the dead was in me, to make this Word that I have been reading a living reality.

I wept for joy.

I was thrilled; Oh, I was thrilled with joy unspeakable.

He was in me!

And He began to take the Jesus things and make them real to my spirit consciousness.

It was like opening up one treasure box after another.

I saw the riches of His glory, of His grace. And it was all mine.

I did not have to struggle to get Wisdom because it was there on tap.

Now I had ability to meet every emergency.

I had strength enough for anything.

I was rich with His riches.

I was redeemed, and I know how to enjoy my freedom.

I was Righteous with His Righteousness, and I began to know what that Righteousness could do for me and enable me to do for others.

Oh, those were glad hours, big hours, rich hours when fellowship took on such a rosy hue that life became very different.

My life was hidden in Him; His life was revealed in me.

I began to know the secret of the Name of Jesus.

I shall never forget the first time I said, "In the Name of Jesus Christ, you are healed." And to see a man that had been in bondage for years become perfectly free and leap up and begin to dance and shout for joy.

I had made a discovery.

No man was ever more thrilled when he discovered gold, than I when I discovered the reality of the ability of the Name of Jesus.

I shall never forget the first time I used His Name with an unsaved person.

He had said, "Mr. Kenyon, I want to be saved, but I just cannot seem to do it. I seem to be bound."

I said, "In the Name of Jesus, I set you free."

That man is preaching the Gospel now. I set him free with the Name of Jesus.

The authority was in the Name.

When I approach the Father in His Name, I can reach the Throne at any time.

"Whatsoever ye shall ask the Father in my name, He will give it to you." Jn. 15:16.

The early church preached the Name and the Word.

We have never done it.

We have preached about the Name, and we preach about the Word, and men write books about the Lord.

They do not mean much to us.

It is the Name, in the lips of love, that breaks the power of the Devil over the broken human.

So we are moving out now into the realm of Life, as sons of liberty.

In the freedom that He has given us, we are enjoying our rights and privileges, and we shout our praises in that marvelous Name.

This is the most striking of all Redemptive truths.

Jesus has met the demands of Justice; He has met the needs of man in Redemption, now He is to meet the needs of the New Creation.

You understand, He entered the Holy of Holies as the High Priest of the New Covenant.

When He sat down, His first office was that of Mediator.

He is the High Priest Mediator between God and man, as natural man cannot approach God.

Jesus is between the natural man and the Holy One upon the Throne.

His Mediatorial Work is the most priceless.

It is what He is doing for us now.

He ever lives to make Intercession for the New Creation.

I have the continual consciousness that there is One who loved me enough to die for me and now lives to pray for me.

If for any reason my prayer is not effectual, His prayer meets my need.

He is not only my Intercessor, but if I get in trouble and the Adversary gains the ascendancy, I have an Advocate with the Father. He is the Lord Advocate for the New Creation.

Chapter XXV

HIS PRESENT DAY MINISTRY

HEN He finished His work in Redemption, He sat down at the Right Hand of the Majesty on High.

His work as Messiah, the Incarnate One and the Member of the Abrahamic Covenant was completed.

He had fulfilled that Covenant.

Its laws, sacrifices, and priesthood were ended in the sight of God.

What a momentous period in Israel's history that was.

It was the beginning of a New Covenant in His blood.

Heb. 8:6-7, "But now hath he obtained a ministry the more excellent, by so much as he is also the mediator of a better covenant, which hath been enacted upon better promises. For if that first covenant had been faultless, then would no place have been sought for a second."

Heb. 8:13, "In that he saith, a new covenant, he hath made the first old. But that which is becoming old and waxeth aged is nigh unto vanishing away."

This New Covenant has a High Priest. Jesus is the High Priest.

It has Sacrifices. Jesus was the major Sacrifice. The Eternal Sacrifice.

Now we have a sacrifice of praise.

Heb. 13:15, "Through him then let us offer up a sacrifice of praise to God continually, that is, the fruit of lips which make confession to his name."

The sacrifice of the First Covenant was the blood of animals. It was poured around the base of the brazen alter.

Our sacrifices are words born of love.

The Old Covenant was for servants; the New Covenant is made up of sons.

The Old Covenant gave to Jehovah a nation; the New Covenant gives to the Father a family.

The Old Covenant headed up in Jehovah; the New Covenant heads up in Jesus the Lord of this Covenant.

John 20:17 tells us that Jesus suddenly appeared to Mary after His Resurrection. When He revealed himself to her, she cried, "Rabboni, my teacher." She fell at His feet; and He said, "touch me not, for I am not yet ascended unto the Father."

He had died a Lamb. He arose a High Priest of the New Covenant.

Heb. 9-12, "Nor yet with the blood of goats and calves but with his own blood, entered in once for all into the holy place, having obtained eternal redemption."

He entered the new Holy of Holies bringing His blood as the new High Priest.

When His blood was accepted, it was possible for God on legal grounds to remit the sins of every person who would accept Christ as Saviour and confess Him as their Lord. When they did this, they received eternal life, making them New Creations.

Heb. 1:3 is a tribute to Jesus and a striking fact of great importance. "Who being the effulgence of his glory, and the very image of his substance, and upholding all things by the word of his power, when he had made purification of sins, sat down on the right hand of the Majesty on High."

This statement is the capping of the climax in regard to the finished work of Christ.

The work had been completed. He sat down. He entered into His rest.

He had met the demands of justice and satisfied them.

He had met the needs of humanity.

God could now claim all who came to Him through Christ, as sons and daughters, on absolutely legal grounds.

Heb. 9:26, "But now once at the end of the ages hath he been manifested to put away sin by the sacrifice of himself."

Sin could not be put away by man. It had to be done by God himself.

Heb. 9:15, "And for this cause he is the mediator of a New Covenant, that a death having taken place for the redemption of the transgressions that were under the first covenant, they that have been called may receive the promise of the eternal inheritance."

You see, He not only died for our sins giving us a standing with God, but He was also dealing with the Sin problem of those under the First Covenant, so that they could receive the promised inheritance.

Jesus is the Mediator

It is vitally important now that we grasp this fact that Jesus is the Mediator of the New Covenant.

Jesus told the disciples in John 14:6, "I am the way, the truth and the life: no one cometh unto the Father, but by me."

Peter preaching to the Jews in Acts 4:12 tells them, "And in none other is there salvation: for neither is there any other name under heaven, that is given among men, wherein we must be saved."

That Name is Jesus.

I Tim. 2:5-6, "For there is one God, one mediator also between God and men, himself man, Christ Jesus, Who gave himself a ransom for all."

How it hurts to hear ignorant men say they are good enough to stand right with God independent of this Mediator.

It makes no difference how religious you are, or how much money you give, or how loudly you preach, if you deny Jesus Christ as the Mediator between God and man you are lost.

Christ is man's only approach to God.

Man must have Eternal Life and there is no receiving Eternal Life but through Jesus Christ.

Christ is man's only Saviour.

I Tim. 4:10, "For to this end we labor and strive, because we have our hope set on the living God, who is the Saviour of all men, specially of them that believe."

Man is spiritually dead, without God and without hope.

He can only find Eternal Life through the one Man Jesus Christ.

Jesus is the Saviour

No man can save himself.

Eph. 2:8, "For by grace are ye saved through faith; and that not of yourselves, it is the gift of God."

This Saviour is God's gift, with Him comes Eternal Life.

It is very important that the heart grasp this fact, Jesus is the Mediator between fallen man and God, when man accepts Him as such He becomes His Saviour, imparting to him Eternal Life, which brings him into the Family of God.

Jesus is the Intercessor

He is now man's Intercessor.

Heb. 7:25, "Wherefore also he is able to save to the uttermost them that draw near unto God through him, seeing he ever liveth to make intercession for them."

It makes no difference how difficult the problem may look to us, we have One seated at the Right Hand of the Father who ever lives to make intercession for us.

As far as we know He has never taken a vacation.

Love has made Him our slave.

He is the Chief of Love Slaves.

Jesus is our Righteousness

Another wonderful truth is that Jesus is our Righteousness. I Cor. 1:30. When we feel unworthy and unfit to approach the Throne we have a Righteous Intercessor who ever lives to pray for us.

This assurance has kept me from feeling discouraged many times during my past years of ministry.

I have become very conscious of the upholding power of the arms of His grace and Intercession.

Paul said, "He loved me and gave Himself up for me."

He caught a glimpse of Love's Intercession at the Right Hand of the Father. It must have melted him. No wonder he so utterly yielded himself to the dominance of the Master.

This Ministry of my Lord at the Right Hand of the Majesty on High is the most priceless truth my heart has ever known.

Jesus is our Advocate

Not only is He our Intercessor, but He is our Advocate.

The New Covenant Advocate is a beautiful title.

He is the Attorney General for the Family of God.

I John 2:1, "My little children, these things write I unto you that ye may not sin. And if any man sin, we have an advocate with the Father, Jesus Christ the righteous."

There are tears in this scripture, tears mingled with joy.

It is one of the most thrilling of all the things written in the New Covenant.

In a previous chapter he has shown you when one steps out of the love realm into the realm of selfishness they sin. When they sin they break fellowship.

This does not mean they break their relationship. They cannot do that, only the One Who made them sons can break this relationship.

We need not worry about committing the unpardonable sin, it is simply that we have been led astray and satisfied the demand of some selfish impulse, thus breaking our fellowship.

I John 1:9, "If we confess our sins, he is faithful and righteous to forgive us our sins, and to cleanse us from all unrighteousness."

It is very important that we understand this fact that the moment we step out of love we step into darkness, and in that darkness "we know not whither we go, for the darkness blinds our eyes."

You see, darkness is the realm of Satan.

I am a child of God, but selfishness has enticed me to leave the realm of love and go over into the realm of darkness or selfishness.

When I do this I lose contact with the Father.

I lose my sense of Righteousness. I need a Righteous Advocate, someone who can step into the Father's presence and take up my case, and restore my lost fellowship.

Isn't it wonderful that He is called the Righteous Advocate, the one who can always stand in the Father's presence for the erring one.

It isn't that we never do wrong.

But it is only when we step out of love that we do wrong.

There is only one real sin for the believer, that is to break the love law.

John 13:34-35, "A new commandment I give unto you, that ye love one another; even as I have loved you, that ye also love one another. By this shall all men know that ye are my disciples (stu-

190

dents) if you have love one to another."

That is not only the badge of the New Creation but the law of the New Creation.

The Father expects us to keep that law as faithfully as Israel kept the Ten Commandments.

You remember that they worshipped the Ten Commandments. They may not have always kept them but they were ever conscious of them.

Wouldn't it be beautiful if we believing sons and daughters of God were always conscious of this New Commandment.

It makes no difference what sin you commit, that sin is stepping out of love.

If we walk in love we never sin.

Jesus is our Lord

He is not only our great Advocate, but He is also our Lord.

We come into the Family by confessing His Lordship.

Rom. 10:9-10, "Because if thou shalt confess with thy mouth Jesus as Lord, and shalt believe in thy heart that God raised him from the dead, thou shalt be saved: for with the heart man believeth unto righteousness; and with the mouth confession is made unto salvation."

Notice that we come into the Family by confessing with our lips the Lordship of this New Creation Man. He is the Head of the New Creation.

He is the first born from among the dead.

Phil. 2:9-11, "Wherefore God also hath highly exalted him, and gave unto him the name which is above every name; That in the name of Jesus every knee should bow . . . And that every tongue should confess that Jesus Christ is Lord, to the glory of God the Father."

When you confess His Lordship, your heart accepts the fact that He automatically becomes your Righteousness. He not only becomes your Righteousness, but you become the Righteousness of God in Him.

That brings you into the closest possible fellowship with the Father.

Through the Son, the Holy Spirit has imparted to you Eternal Life, the nature of the Father.

Now you are a child by nature; you are an heir of God, a joint heir with Jesus Christ.

You ask, "What does this Lordship mean?"

Why it means that He is your Protector, your Shepherd, the Lord of the New Creation, the Caretaker of the New Creation.

The 23rd Psalm describes Him. "Jehovah is my Shepherd, I shall not want."

You know that the Jehovah of the Old Covenant is the Jesus of the New.

He is the same yesterday, today and forever.

He is the Lord of the three tenses.

The past, present and future tenses.

What He was yesterday, He is today and what He is today, He will be tomorrow.

As your Mediator, He brought you into vital union with the Father; as Intercessor, He ever lives to pray for you; as your Advocate, He protects you against the enemy: as your Lord, He is your supply, to meet every need of yours.

You can say with Paul, Phil. 4:11, "Not that I speak in respect of want: for I have learned, in whatsoever state I am, therein to be independent of circumstances." And that wonderful thirteenth verse, "I can do all things in him that strengtheneth me."

The 19th verse, "And my God shall supply every need of yours according to his riches in glory in Christ Jesus."

The wealth of Heaven is ours.

The wealth of Love is at our disposal.

Jesus gave us instructions in the Sermon on the Mount.

Matt. 6:30-34, He climaxed it with "But seek ye first his kingdom and his righteousness; and all these things shall be added unto you.

The kingdom had not yet come.

Righteousness was not yet available.

They had not yet been born again.

Notice Rom. 10:11, "Whosoever believeth on him shall not be put to shame."

Another translation is "Whosoever believeth on Him shall not wander about distractedly," looking for another Protector, Saviour or Lord.

Of all the promises given in the Pauline Revelation, to me this is the most priceless, that we shall not be put to shame.

There is not power enough in all this selfish world to sever, injure or hinder the fruit bearing of one branch of this vine.

I can say, "great peace have they who love the Master. Nothing shall offend them."

You can rest in absolute security in His protecting care.

He cannot overlook or forget you are tied to Him, just as a branch is tied to the vine.

Jesus is the New Covenant Surety

Heb. 7:21-22, "The Lord sware and will not repent himself, Thou art a priest for ever; by so much also has Jesus become the surety of a better covenant."

I know of no scripture that thrills my heart more.

This One sat down at the Right Hand of the Majesty on High, when He had completed His work, to become the Mediator.

As soon as we find Christ as Saviour and receive Eternal Life, He becomes our Intercessor, and then the Advocate, He is our Lord, and now we look at Him as the Surety, the Guarantor of the New Covenant.

The Throne is back of every Word from Matthew to Revelation XXII.

Jesus, the Father, and the Holy Spirit are back of the Throne.

Now the heart can rest in His love.

How many times I have whispered Luke 1:37, "For no word from God shall be void of ability in fulfillment." Or "I watch over my word to perform it."

Or Is. 55:11, "So shall my word be that goeth forth out of my mouth: it shall not return unto me void, but it shall accomplish that which I please, and it shall prosper in the thing whereto I sent it."

His word cannot be broken so I rest with a quiet assurance.

Gen. 22:17, "That in blessing I will bless thee, and in multiplying I will multiply thy seed as the stars of the heaven, and as the sand which is upon the sea shore; and thy seed shall possess the gate of his enemies."

As Jehovah was back of that first Covenant Jesus is back of this New Covenant.

Is. 42:6 is a remarkable statement, "I Jehovah, have called thee in righteousness, and will hold thy hand, and will keep thee, and give thee for a covenant of the people, for a light of the Gentiles."

750 years before He came He was promised to be the Covenant.

He became the Covenant Lamb; the Covenant Sacrifice that Israel offered upon the cross.

My heart can see how He loves me, He died for me, and He ever lives for me.

Jesus is the High Priest

The High Priestly ministry of the Master at the Right Hand of the Father is the most priceless.

He offered His own blood as the basis of this New Covenant.

He is the great High Priest Who makes our worship and love acceptable to the Father.

No truth of life is more thrillingly priceless than this.

You can see now that the work of Christ was first for us as a Sin Substitute; then in us through the Word by the Holy Spirit, building the very nature and life of Christ into our inner beings, making this hidden man of the heart a fit companion for the Master.

But that would be incomplete if He did not have a ministry for the sons of God now.

So the most vital of all teachings is the ministry given in this chapter. Read it over and over until your heart takes it in, and you know that He ever lives for you, that He loves you and bears you upon His shoulders before the Father.

Read Eph. 2:6, "And raised us up with him, and made us to sit with him in the heavenly places, in Christ Jesus."

Your Lord is there; your Father is there; your name is inscribed there and you are there as a member of that new Body of which Christ is the Head.

≡Ⅲ≡Ⅲ≡Ⅲ≡Ⅲ≡Ⅲ≡Ⅲ≡Ⅲ≡Ⅲ≡Ⅲ≡Ⅲ≡Ⅲ≡Ⅲ≡Ⅲ≡Ⅲ≡Ⅲ≡Ⅲ≡Ⅲ

My heart is thrilled as I go from scene to scene with the Man of the cross, the Resurrection, and the Throne.

We have seen Him seated at the Right Hand of the Majesty on High after the completion of the Eternal Redemption.

Now we come to the close and give you this final chapter, "The Father's Care."

Somehow the heart goes back over these momentous days of the great Substitution and in letters of transcendent light, we see these words, "God so loved the world."

If He loved the world that was held in captivity by Satanic nature, how He must love those whom He has Redeemed and Recreated; those who have received His own nature, His own substance and Being.

He has now Recreated them and made them His own sons and daughters.

If He loved them enough to give His Son as a Substitute for them while they were still His enemies, who can measure His love for them now as sons and daughters.

They are in the Beloved.

They are a part of Him.

It is His joy to care for them and comfort them.

He is love and they are His own.

Jesus said, "If a man love me he will keep my word, and the Father and I will love him and come and make our home with him."

I can hear Him whisper, "Cast all your anxiety on me for I am caring for you."

≡Ⅲ≡Ⅲ≡Ⅲ≡Ⅲ≡Ⅲ≡Ⅲ≡Ⅲ≡Ⅲ≡Ⅲ≡Ⅲ≡Ⅲ≡Ⅲ≡Ⅲ≡Ⅲ≡Ⅲ≡Ⅲ≡Ⅲ

Chapter XXVI

THE FATHER'S CARE

O TRUTH is so far-reaching as this blessed fact, that our Father cares for us.

He was just Elohim, El Shaddai, and Jehovah to Israel. He was shut up in the Holy of Holies.

He dealt in awful judgment to the law breakers and disobedient. They did not know Him as a Father. They did not know Him as a lover.

They were commanded to love and obey Him or suffer the consequences.

Then into this hard, harsh, atmosphere of justice, Jesus came. They could not understand Him.

He talked about their God as His Father.

He told of the Father's love, the Father's care for His own.

It mystified them.

If He had come with a message like John the Baptist, commanding them to repent, calling them bitter names that they had to acknowledge were true, they would have understood it. When He introduced a lover, a Father-God of love, His words fell upon unresponsive ears.

Notice these scriptures and you will admit that we, as sons and daughters of this Father-God have never seen this love side.

Jn. 16:23, "And in that day ye shall ask me nothing. Verily, verily, I say unto you, if ye shall ask anything of the Father, He will give it you in my name."

Jn. 16:27, "For the Father Himself loveth you."

Matt. 6:8, "Your Heavenly Father knoweth what things ye have need of, before ye ask Him. After this manner therefore pray: Our Father ...."

Notice the utter tenderness of it.

Listen to the Master again: (26th verse) "Behold the birds of the heaven, that they sow not, neither do they reap, nor gather into barns; and your heavenly Father feedeth them. Are ye not of much more value than they?"

They never grasped it. That was utterly new.

It is new to most of our church members today. Most of us have been taught to fear and shrink from a God of justice.

Verses 30-33: "But if God doth so clothe the grass of the field, which today is, and tomorrow is cast into the oven, shall he not much more clothe you, O ye of little faith? Be not therefore anxious saying, What shall we eat? or, What shall we drink? or, Wherewithal shall we be clothed? For after all these things do the Gentiles seek; for your heavenly Father knoweth that ye have need of all these things.

But seek ye first His kingdom and His Righteousness; and all these things shall be added unto you."

The Father cares for His own.

34th verse: "Be not therefore anxious for the morrow."

Have no worry, no fret, no anxiety.

Your heavenly Father knoweth that ye have need of these things.

If He is your Father, you may be assured that He will take a Father's place and perform a Father's part.

You may be certain if He is your Father, that He loves you and will care for you.

Jn. 14:23, "If a man love me, he will keep my word: and my Father will love him, and we will come unto him, and make our abode with Him.

This is a revelation of the Father's attitude toward His own children.

21st verse, "He that hath my commandments, and keepeth them, he it is that loves me: and he shall be loved of my Father, and I will love him, and will manifest myself unto him."

Two things are suggested here:

"He that keepeth my commandments." His commandments are "that we love one another, even as He loved us."

The second fact: "He shall be loved of my Father."

If you walk in love, you walk in God's realm.

This great Father God is a love Father.

His very nature compells Him to care for us and protect us and shield us.

Our relation as sons and daughters is a challenge to His love.

We hold the same relation to Him that Jesus did when He walked the earth.

Jn. 15:1: "I am the true vine, and my Father is the husband-man."

The Father is the husbandman. He is the caretaker, the protector, the shield, the sustainer, the trainer, and the educator.

As they train the branches of a vine, so He trains the branches of this body of Christ.

He is love.

When He tells us to walk in love, it means to walk in Him.

Jn. 17:23: "I in them, and thou in me, that they may be perfected into one; that the world may know that thou didst send me, and lovedst them, even as thou lovedst me."

If He loves me as He loved Jesus, I am not afraid to face life's problems, because He is with me.

He was with the Master.

Jn. 16:32: "I am not alone, because the Father is with me."

What Jesus said about the Father's relation to Him is true of His relation and attitude toward you and me.

Jn. 16:27: "For the Father Himself loveth you, because ye have loved me, and have believed that I came forth from the Father."

Nothing could be stronger than this or more comforting, that the Father Himself knows you, loves you, longs to bless you.

These scriptures belong to us:

I Pet. 5:7: "Casting all your anxiety upon Him, for He careth for you."

This is the Father's message to your heart.

He wants you to end worry and fear and doubt and to abandon yourself to His care and love.

Phil. 4:6: "In nothing be anxious," or "Be careful for nothing."

Your heavenly Father wants to walk with you as He walked with Jesus when He was here on earth.

Phil. 4:13: "I can do all things in Him that strengtheneth me.

You can do anything.

You can rise to the place where you are unafraid in the most unpleasant circumstances, because your Father is on your side.

Rom. 8:31: "If God is for us, who is against us?"

The Father's love compels Him to care for us.

When you come to know His love and swing free in that love, all doubts and fears will be destroyed.

The Father's love for you is of no value, if it is not known.

If it is known and not acted upon, it is of no value.

It is truth acted upon that brings dividends to the heart.

You must learn to trust in Him with all your heart and to stop leaning upon your own understanding.

You must move out of the Sense Knowledge realm into the realm of the spirit.

Prov. 3:5-6: "Trust in Jehovah with all thy heart, And lean not upon shine own understanding: In all thy ways acknowledge Him, And He will direct thy paths."

Ps. 27:1: Jehovah is my light and my salvation, whom shall I fear? Jehovah is the strength of my life, of whom shall I be afraid?"

He is your light.

He is your deliverance.

He is the strength of your life.

There is nothing to fear.

What can man do to the man whom God loves and protects?

Satan saw that when he said: "You have built a hedge around Job, so I cannot reach him." Job. 1:10.

The Father builds a hedge around those who love Him and walk with Him.

Ps. 36:9: "For with thee is the fountain of life: In thy light shall we see light." God is the fountain of life, of strength.

He is your fountain.

He is your light.

In that light you see His will and come to know it.

Ps. 34:7: "The angel of Jehovah encampeth round about them that fear Him, And delivereth them."

That is the Father's message to you.

Notice the 9th and 10th verses:

"Oh fear Jehovah, ye His saints; For there is no want to them that fear Him. The young lions do lack, and suffer hunger; But they that seek Jehovah shall not want any good thing."

Ps. 125:1-2: "They that trust in Jehovah are as Mount Zion, which cannot be moved, but abideth forever. As the mountains are round about Jerusalem, So Jehovah is round about His people From this time forth and forevermore."

Is. 43:1-2: "Fear not, for I have redeemed thee; I have called thee by thy name, thou art mine. When thou passest through the waters, I will be with thee; and through the rivers, they shall not overflow thee: when thou walkest through the fire, thou shalt not be burned, neither shall the flame kindle upon thee."

That is your Father talking.

Hear Him whisper again (and there is no message that is sweeter): Is. 41:10: "Fear thou not, for I am with thee; be not dismayed, for I am thy God; I will strengthen thee; yea, I will help thee; yea, I will uphold thee with the right hand of my righteousness."

Notice He says to you, "Fear thou not, for I am with thee."

In the previous verse He said: "I have chosen thee and not cast thee away."

How His heart reaches after us.

He does not want us to fear any longer, for the Creator is with us.

"Be not dismayed." Don't be afraid of anything.

They can't conquer you.

He is caring for you.

He will meet your needs.

Phil. 4:19: "My God shall supply every need of yours according to His riches in glory in Christ Jesus."

This is not religion. This is not preaching. This is a living truth from the heart of the Father to you.

"Be not dismayed, for I am thy God."

He knows who He is.

He knows that He created the universe by the word of His power.

He knows His ability.

He knows He can conquer your enemies and overcome the circumstances that surround your life.

"I will strengthen thee."

This is God's strength and ability for you.

No wonder Paul, speaking of this very subject in II Cor. 3.5

said: "For our sufficiency is of God; who also made us sufficient as ministers of a new covenant."

God's ability becomes your ability.

Phil. 2:13: "For it is God who is at work with you, willing and working His own good pleasure."

It is your Father energizing your mind, supplementing your weakness with His strength.

Eph. 3:16: "That He would grant you, according to the riches of His glory, that ye may be strengthened with power through His Spirit in the inward man."

God's ability is in you.

20th verse, "Now unto Him that is able to do exceeding abundantly above all we ask or think, according to the power that worketh in us."

It is according to God's ability in you.

Your Father's care is the most priceless gift that heaven ever gave since sonship became yours.

Your Father is watching over you.

He is caring for you, listening to your call.

He is your helper.

What more can you ask if He is upholding you with the right hand of His Righteousness?

That right hand is Jesus.

He is upholding you with Jesus, with His very life and strength.

I Cor. 6:19: "Or know ye not that your body is a temple of the Holy Spirit which is in you, which ye have from God? and ye are not your own."

God comes into our bodies, makes His home, lives in them so He can speak through our voice, think through our minds, love through our hearts, make Himself absolutely one with us, swallowing up our very weakness with His strength.

He absorbs our inefficiency with His sufficiency.

Our privileges cannot be estimated.

This indwelling fact is the most amazing fact of the human experience.

There is no passage that describes the Father's and Jesus' love attitude toward us more beautifully than Ps. 23:1:

"Jehovah is my shepherd, I shall not want."

This is perfect satisfaction.

This is finding the ultimate of living, "I shall not want."

It is beyond our understanding. It is in the realm of the spirit.

"He maketh me to lie down in green pastures."

This is where the luscious clover and tender grasses carpet the ground.

There is no effort required here to get enough.

He not only causes me to go into the green pastures, but He

leads me beside the waters of gentle stillness.

Water and food are the requisites that sustain life.

He maketh me to lie down and rest in safety and quietness in the pastures of plenty. Near me is a babbling brook. Its living waters answer the cry of my heart.

I have water, I have food. I have protection. I have shelter. I have His care. This is my Father.

When I am frightened and filled with fear, my whole being is convulsed with agony, "He restoreth my soul."

He keeps me quiet.

He makes me normal again.

He brushes away my fears and anxieties and He holds me to His breast and breathes into me His own courage and faith. My heart laughs at my enemies.

For He guideth me down the paths of grace, into the realm of Righteousness, where I stand in His presence as though sin had never been, where I romp and play in the throne room of grace with never a thought of fear or dread.

My Father is the one who is on the throne.

He may be the judge of the world. He may be God to the sinner, but He is my own Father.

He loves me and cares for me.

Matt. 6:32: "For your heavenly Father knoweth that ye have need of all these things," rings through my soul. I have it framed and hanging in memory's chamber so as to remind me morning by morning that my Father is watching over me.

This would not be perfect unless we read, Jn. 10:29: "My Father who hath given them unto me is greater than all." We have never majored this Father fact. It is coming to the front to meet the heart needs in this dark period of human suffering.

The God who is upon the throne is your Father.

The one whom you feared and worshipped from afar is your Father.

He is asking you to draw near to His throne of love gifts, that He may pour out upon you the riches of His love and grace to meet every need of yours.

Heb. 4:16: "Let us therefore draw near with boldness unto the throne of grace, that we may receive mercy and may find grace to help us in time of need."

THE BOOK IS READ

What has it done for you?

One said who read the manuscript, "That book should be read by the leaders of our Nation."

What do you say?

What will you do?

See that your friends have a copy.

Be a fruit bearing branch!

Inspiring Books by E. W. KENYON

THE BIBLE IN THE LIGHT
OF OUR REDEMPTION
    A Basic Bible Course

ADVANCED BIBLE COURSE
    Studies in the Deeper Life

THE HIDDEN MAN OF THE HEART

WHAT HAPPENED
    From the Cross to the Throne

NEW CREATIONS REALITIES

IN HIS PRESENCE
    The Secret of Prayer

THE TWO KINDS OF LIFE

THE FATHER AND HIS FAMILY
    The Story of Man's Redemption

THE WONDERFUL NAME OF JESUS
    Our Rights and Privileges in Prayer

JESUS THE HEALER
    Has Brought Healing to Thousands

KENYON'S LIVING POEMS

THE NEW KIND OF LOVE

THE TWO KINDS OF FAITH

THE TWO KINDS OF RIGHTEOUSNESS

THE BLOOD COVENANT

THE TWO KINDS OF KNOWLEDGE

SIGN POSTS ON THE ROAD TO SUCCESS

IDENTIFICATION

Order From:
KENYON'S GOSPEL PUBLISHING SOCIETY
P.O. Box 973, Lynnwood, Washington 98046-0973
Website: www.kenyons.org